REIMAGINING ARCHITECTURAL DRAWING
PRINT AND PROCESS

Guest-edited by Mark Dorrian, Riet Eeckhout, and Arnaud Hendrickx

03 | 95 | 2025

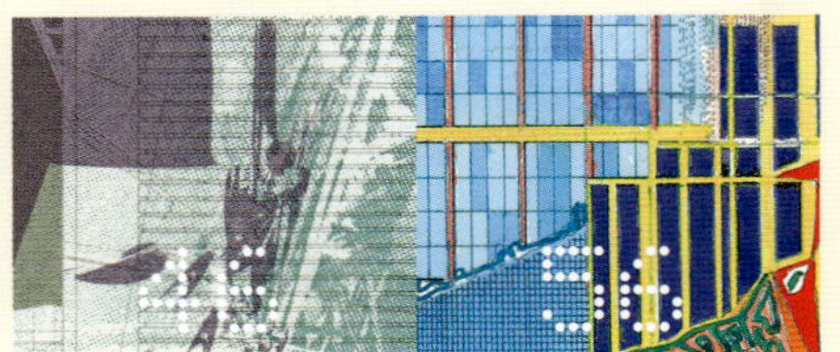

ISSN 0003-8504

ISBN 978-1-966515-00-5

◭ ARCHITECTURAL DESIGN   DECEMBER 2025   VOLUME 95 | ISSUE 03

Editorial Offices
Axiomatic Editions, an imprint of ORO Editions
250 Bowery
New York, New York 10012

Editorial Director
Ashley Simone

Editor
Neil Spiller

Managing Editor
Caroline Ellerby

Contributing Editor
Abigail Grater

Publisher
Gordon Goff

Assistant Production Editor
Sarah Fingerhood

Design
Artmedia Ltd, London

Front cover
Metis: Mark Dorrian + Adrian Hawker with
Richard Collins, digital extracts and texture
mapping, Storm Gallery, 2024
© Metis (Mark Dorrian + Adrian Hawker)

Inside front cover
Metis: Mark Dorrian + Adrian Hawker, Storm
Fold 3: a new Risograph print, Storm Gallery,
2025
© Metis (Mark Dorrian + Adrian Hawker)

Page 1
Bryan Cantley, 6TH ST. Artifact 11, 2024.
© Bryan Cantley

Disclaimer
The Publisher and Editors cannot
be held responsible for errors or
any consequences arising from the
use of information contained in this
journal; the views and opinions
expressed do not necessarily reflect
those of the Publisher and Editors.

Journal Customer Services
For ordering information, claims, and any
enquiry concerning your journal subscription
please go to www.archdesignjournal.com

Print ISBN: 978-1-966515-00-5
Print ISSN: 0003-8504
Online ISSN: 1554-2769

Institutional
$950   print and online
$850   print only
$850   online only

Individual
$190   print and online
$160   print only
$120   online only

Individual issues
$40

All prices are subject to change without notice.

MARK DORRIAN, RIET EECKHOUT, AND ARNAUD HENDRICKX

Mark Dorrian, **Riet Eeckhout**, and **Arnaud Hendrickx** are scholars and practitioners interested in the culture and history of architectural drawing, its contemporary forms, and, more generally, the relation between mark-making and speculative thinking. Their collaboration began with a project initiated by Eeckhout and Hendrickx in 2018, which gathered a group of architects, renowned for their drawn production, together in a series of meetings at which they presented and discussed their work. The records of these were published as the book *Drawing Architecture: Conversations on Contemporary Practice* (Lund Humphries, 2022), co-edited by Dorrian, Eeckhout, and Hendrickx. This *Δ* extends the project in its documentation of a collaboration with the A83 gallery and printmaking studio in New York, which foregrounded questions of transmediality, artifactual agency, and the restlessly fissive powers of the archive.

Mark Dorrian holds the Forbes Chair in Architecture at the University of Edinburgh, Scotland, is Co-Director of Metis, and Editor-in-Chief of *Drawing Matter Journal*. His work spans topics in architecture and urbanism, art history and theory, and media studies, and has appeared in journals including *Cabinet*, *Log*, *Radical Philosophy*, and *Word & Image*. His books include: *Metis: Urban Cartographies* (Black Dog, 2002), co-authored with Adrian Hawker; and *Seeing From Above: The Aerial View in Visual Culture* (2013), co-edited with Frédéric Pousin, and *Writing on the Image: Architecture, the City and the Politics of Representation* (2015), both published by I.B. Tauris. He has been a visiting professor at schools in Europe, the US, and China, and has received awards from the Canadian Centre for Architecture (CCA) in Montréal, the Department of Prints & Drawings at the British Museum, and the Graham Foundation, Chicago.

Riet Eeckhout is an architect and Associate Professor at the Faculty of Architecture, KU Leuven, Belgium. Her research on drawing architecture investigates the critical and generative potential of drawings beyond mere representation within architectural practice. She exhibits, lectures, and publishes on drawing as a mode of architectural research. Her drawings have been shown internationally, including at the Venice Architecture Biennale; Galerie d'Architecture, Paris; Tchoban Foundation and the Museum of Architectural Drawing, Berlin; Architekturmuseum der TU Berlin; Design Centre UQAM, Montréal; and Art Omi: Architecture, New York.

Arnaud Hendrickx is an architect and Professor of Architectural Design at the Faculty of Architecture, KU Leuven—Campus Sint-Lucas Brussels, where he currently serves as program director of the Master of Architecture. His work explores the intersection of architecture, art, and exhibition practices, and as part of this he co-leads Architectuur Voor en Door Als Kunst (AVDAK), an academic design office exploring exhibition scenography and architectural representation. He contributed to the Luxembourg Pavilion at the Venice Architecture Biennale in 2021, and he is the author of the book *René Heyvaert: Denver Mosaic 1961* (Roma Publications, 2022).

Transference

… a print is a rather bizarre thing—a thing that is born from a moment of dark and mysterious contact under intense pressure, in a drama full of inversion and reversal and blindness and uncertainty.
— Jennifer L. Roberts, *Contact: Art and the Pull of Print*, 2024[1]

On February 14, 2025, a group of people sat down to eat at a long table in a gallery in SoHo, New York. The opening of an exhibition had just ended and now only those directly involved in the show remained—exhibitors, curators, assistants, and associates of one kind or another. The table at which they gathered was an unusual one. Below its transparent surface was a recessed lower plane, on which an array of prints and print-related artifacts were displayed. The set-up acted as a metaphor for the print process itself—for onto the receptive surfaces below fell the shadows of plates, cutlery, glasses, bottles, and napkins, as well as the splashes, smears, and marks that would accumulate as the evening wore on.

The materials onto which these shadows were cast, which included works by Morphosis, Michael Graves, Aldo Rossi, and Venturi, Rauch & Scott Brown, were all related to what was displayed around the walls of the gallery—a sequence of new prints that had been produced for the show, together with associated drawings, constructions, optical devices, and the like. In addition to these, an orange cloth-bound folio was displayed, brightly lit, at the gallery entrance. This was a limited-edition box set of 16 prints produced by the gallery on the occasion of the exhibition. In a smaller back room, its contents—with a few exceptions 12 x 12 inch Risograph prints—were unboxed and displayed around the walls.

Mark Dorrian, Riet Eeckhout, and Arnaud Hendrickx

Passages Between Prints and Drawings

A Short History of an Idea

The event and exhibition, which was titled "The Sixth Somewhat Annual Meeting" and ran until March 21 at the nonprofit A83 gallery and printmaking studio at Grand Street, was the latest manifestation of a series of activities that stretch back to 2018. That year Riet Eeckhout and Arnaud Hendrickx of KU Leuven in Belgium initiated a project to engage a series of contemporary practitioners and writers interested in exploratory forms of architectural drawing. The intention was to establish a forum at which work could be presented, slowly reflected upon, and expansively discussed in a way that went beyond the possibilities typically offered in the academy or in practice. With a working title of "Drawing Conversations," the first meeting was held in April 2019 in New York and the second in London later the same year. They would continue across the ensuing Covid-19 pandemic, although now necessarily online.

Stages in the Risograph printing of Neil Spiller's *Handler of Gravity,* A83 printmaking studio, New York, 2025

Four prints hang side by side to dry, each showing a successive layer in the overprinting process. From left to right, the image builds in complexity and depth as additional colors are applied, revealing the cumulative logic of the medium.

At these gatherings, specific drawings were shown and described by their producers, and the open discussions that followed were recorded and transcribed. These transcripts would in turn form the basis of a book, *Drawing Architecture: Conversations on Contemporary Practice*, that was published in 2022.[2] Although including introductory texts and interpretive essays, the book mostly adopts a dialogical script-like format, the intention being to convey the dynamic character of the exchanges and the particularity of the terms through which the participants vocalized their work and operative concepts.

At the same time, the project was moving to expand its circle of interlocutors. This led to the exhibition "Drawing Conversations / Autour du dessin" held at the Design Centre of the Université du Québec à Montréal (UQAM), from September 15 to November 6, 2022, at which 56 works were displayed, accompanied by curated interviews in audio and printed formats.[3] This was also the point at which a conversation with Owen Nichols and Clara Syme, co-directors of A83, began around the idea that participants in the project each select an artifact from the John Nichols Printmakers & Publishers Collection, which is located at the gallery, in order to develop a new print-based work in relation to it. Owen's father, John, opened his printmaking studio in 1978. It ran for 16 years, producing images for key US architectural practices of the period and accumulating a remarkable archive that includes finished and test prints, transparencies and lithographic plates, and diverse materials produced as by-products of specific printing processes. In early February 2023, some of the group traveled to New York to explore the archive and participate in a discussion at the Cooper Union. From there the project with A83 gathered pace, further focused by a series of UK-based meetings in October

The silkscreen table at the
A83 printmaking studio,
New York,
2025

opposite left: On its surface rests a screen bearing
one layer of *The Phantoms of A83* by CJ Lim.
With two "eyes" seemingly staring from the
photosensitive emulsion, the table takes on an
anthropomorphic quality—as if the tools themselves
possess a personality. This very setup is the origin
for many of the works featured in "The Sixth
Somewhat Annual Meeting," its accompanying folio
Records of the Sixth Somewhat Annual Meeting,
and, ultimately, this issue of *D*.

Owen Nichols at work in the
A83 printmaking studio,
New York,
2025

opposite right: Black ink is carefully pulled through
the mesh to produce a layer of *Isovist Path Analysis*
by Arnaud Hendrickx. The scene captures the
precision, physical effort, and irreversibility that
define the manual silkscreening process.

The opening night of "The Sixth Somewhat
Annual Meeting" exhibition, A83 gallery,
New York,
February 14, 2025

above: As the public drifted out, those directly
involved in the show gathered around a long
table. Beneath its clear surface lay prints from the
archive; above it, wine, conversation, and the slow
accumulation of stains, crumbs, and glass rings.
The scene became a living print—an accidental
overlay of gestures, matter, and memory.

the same year—at the Bartlett School of Architecture in London,
Drawing Matter in Somerset, and the University of Edinburgh
(where the extraordinary drawings of marine organisms produced
as part of the late 19th-century oceanographic survey known as
the Challenger Expedition were viewed, alongside other activities).

This *D* issue, then, presents a documentation and series of
critical reflections on the works produced in the context of the
A83 project. In doing this, it follows a similar format to an earlier
issue, published in 2022, which disseminated the work of the
group. Titled "Radical Architectural Drawing," this was structured
through a sequence of discrete essays by invited writers that, taken
together, presented a diverse and multi-perspectival array of ways
of thinking about the drawn work.[4]

Printworks

The work documented here is the first by the group in which the context is a common project. It is, moreover, a very particular one—one that brought long-standing preoccupations with drawing into contact with the tools, materials, and procedures of printmaking. Furthermore, it took shape as an engagement with the archive as a repository of artifacts that were both objects embedded in particular disciplinary histories and ineluctably material things, subject to their own, often surprising, transformations and adventures. During the group's visit to the archive, techniques were discussed and prints variously scrutinized—held to the light, examined from the back, viewed through magnifying devices, scratched and sniffed. This kind of expansive attention opened ways of reading the archival materials in non-normative ways and the first anticipation of the often-unexpected routes via which they might come to animate new works. The encounter with remarkable prints such as the silkscreen of Morphosis's 6th Street Residence (Santa Monica, California, 1987–92), discussed by Morphosis founder Thom Mayne in this issue, gave rise to questions of disciplinary indebtedness and what it means to work in relation to such artifacts, acting upon them while honoring their example.

A commitment to drawing as a locus of emergence had been important in the group's earlier discussions, and now this met with the logic and processes of printmaking. This affected not only how works were prepared, but also what they came to be as they were re-instantiated in different media, sometimes as discrete stages in a process—in, for example, photo-exposed screens, one for each color separation, part-objects that exuded their own spectral presence. Participants saw their work transforming as it was reformulated across different print-media artifacts, test-printed onto different papers, and sometimes amalgamated with other images in sedimentations of printed layers. It became difficult to know where authorship started and stopped, as it was increasingly complicated through negotiations with the reference artifacts and by the procedures of printmaking.

Perhaps most striking of all was the revelation in the first encounter with the printed object. This was, to some extent, due to the physical distance between those involved, but it is also innate to a process that the art historian Jennifer L. Roberts beautifully characterizes: "the moment of printing is radically invisible. The actual formation of the print occurs in a tight, unobservable space. The print is made darkly … no one can watch it; no one can surveil it. This helps explain the mystique of the 'pull' in printmaking; that moment when the image is peeled away from the matrix, revealing it to the eye and to the air for the first time … It is released into light, into space, into the range of the aerial and the optical."[5]

Goldleafing of Arnaud Hendrickx's
Isovist Path Analysis,
A83 printmaking studio,
New York,
2025

Application of gold leaf to the reverse side of a transparent acrylic sheet, part of *Isovist Path Analysis* by Arnaud Hendrickx. The image highlights the delicacy of the material and the collaborative craftsmanship involved in the production of the works—one of many distinctive techniques employed throughout the exhibition "The Sixth Somewhat Annual Meeting."

Superposition of test prints, A83
printmaking studio,
New York,
2025

Elements from *Hedge with floating shadow
peepshow and floating picture plane* by
Nat Chard overlap with registration marks
and colored layers from Shaun Murray's
Ineffaceable Illuminations. A by-product of
the screenprinting process, this composite
image reveals the medium's capacity for
serendipitous encounters.

Matters Arising

The articles in this issue are by a diverse array of authors, including a psychoanalyst, an anthropologist, and a philosopher, as well as architectural scholars. It opens with Paddi Alice Benson's commentary on Metis, the practice of Mark Dorrian and Adrian Hawker, who worked upon—and directly printed from—a flood-damaged pile of sedimented silkscreen transparencies, originally produced for the printing of the plans of Venturi, Rauch & Scott Brown's Sainsbury Wing of the National Gallery in London (1991). Writing, among much else, of "wandering boundaries," her piece tracks the peregrinations of this very material pile of drawings across various media forms. Following this, Jason Lee explores what he describes as CJ Lim's "architectural ghost story." Lim's work, Lee tells us, summons spirits from the archive, his revenants (figurations of Bernard Tschumi, Aldo Rossi, and Frank Gehry) embossed under great pressure into thick moistened paper, which is then overprinted with fluorescent ink. Thom Mayne's text on Bryan Cantley is a unique case in which the author of the original archival artifact (the *6th Street Residence* print) responds to its reimagining. Cantley's work, Mayne argues, draws architecture beyond an "orthographic tradition" in the service of built form into a condition in which architecture is no longer a discrete object supported by—and separable from—graphic and informational codes, but rather mingles with and is distributed through them. Riet Eeckhout chose also to work in relation to a Morphosis print—or rather, in her case, two. Aleksandra Wagner's article, which evolves as a kind of dialogue with Eeckhout, gives us an intense reflection on questions of working in the wake of another, of depth and immersion, and of the conditions under which something can be said to "finish."

Michael Webb,
Drive-in House three-phase plan projection
with rudimentary solar path diagram,
1993

right: Proposal for a combination rotating garage/house in emulation of the elegant movements of the Wankel rotary engine. Phase 1: car has just entered garage, intake tube and driver's line of vision (white line) are in vertical alignment; Phase 2: house shown as rotating around the driver's center of vision (the car doors begin to open [not shown]); Phase 3: car has rotated fully into the living area of the house, its doors are open with their internal form extending the wall surfaces of the room into which they fit.

Perry Kulper,
"Speculative Rooftop House," Kimono, plan,
2020

below: Surrounded by a retractable 30-foot-high orange curtain, this theatrically inspired, reclusive, and promiscuous house "floats" above an atmospherically rich turquoise-clad bowstring truss roof. Made of large structural steel "baskets," an empty elliptical pool, a burnt-wood kitchen, a cast-rubber powder room, manicured grass peacock "feathers," milled wooden decks, and a kimono-inspired roof, its highly varied spatial setup prompts the invigoration of other forgotten urban spaces, while structuring the possibility of unique domestic practices.

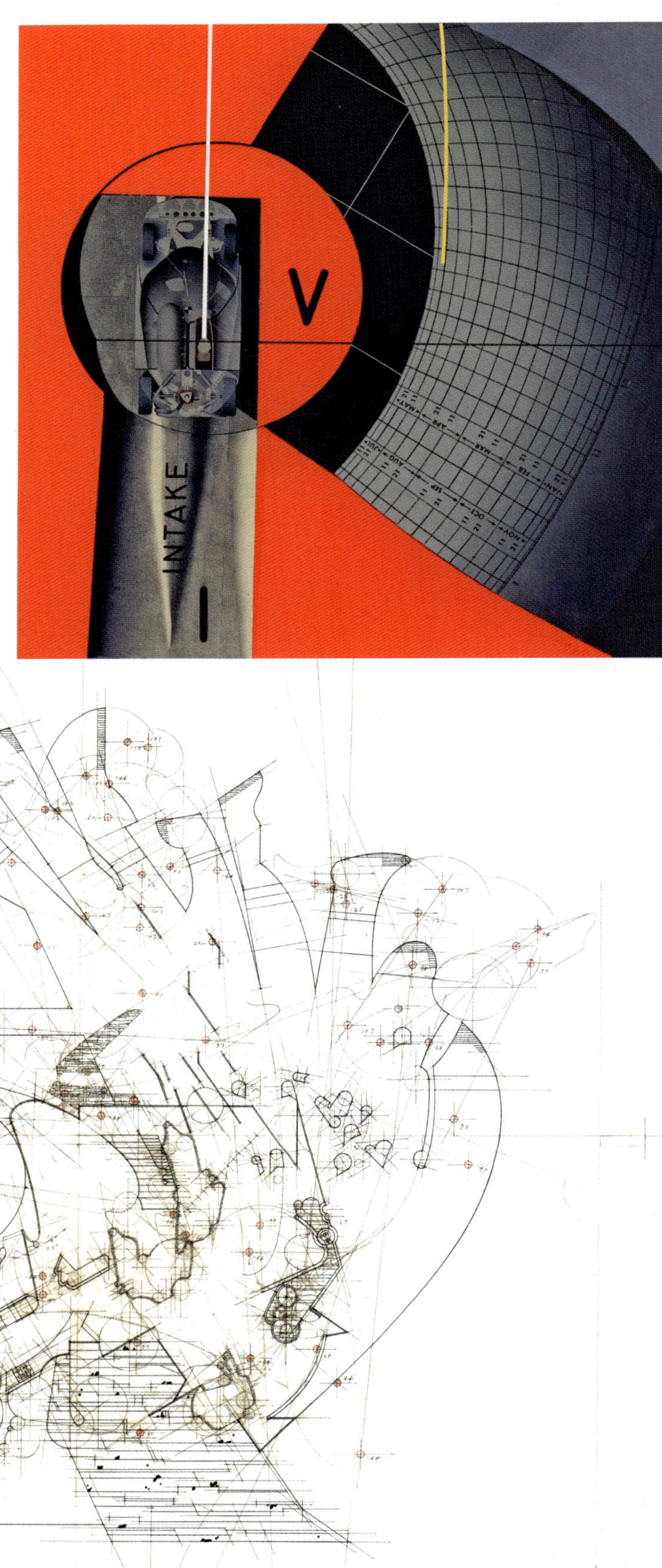

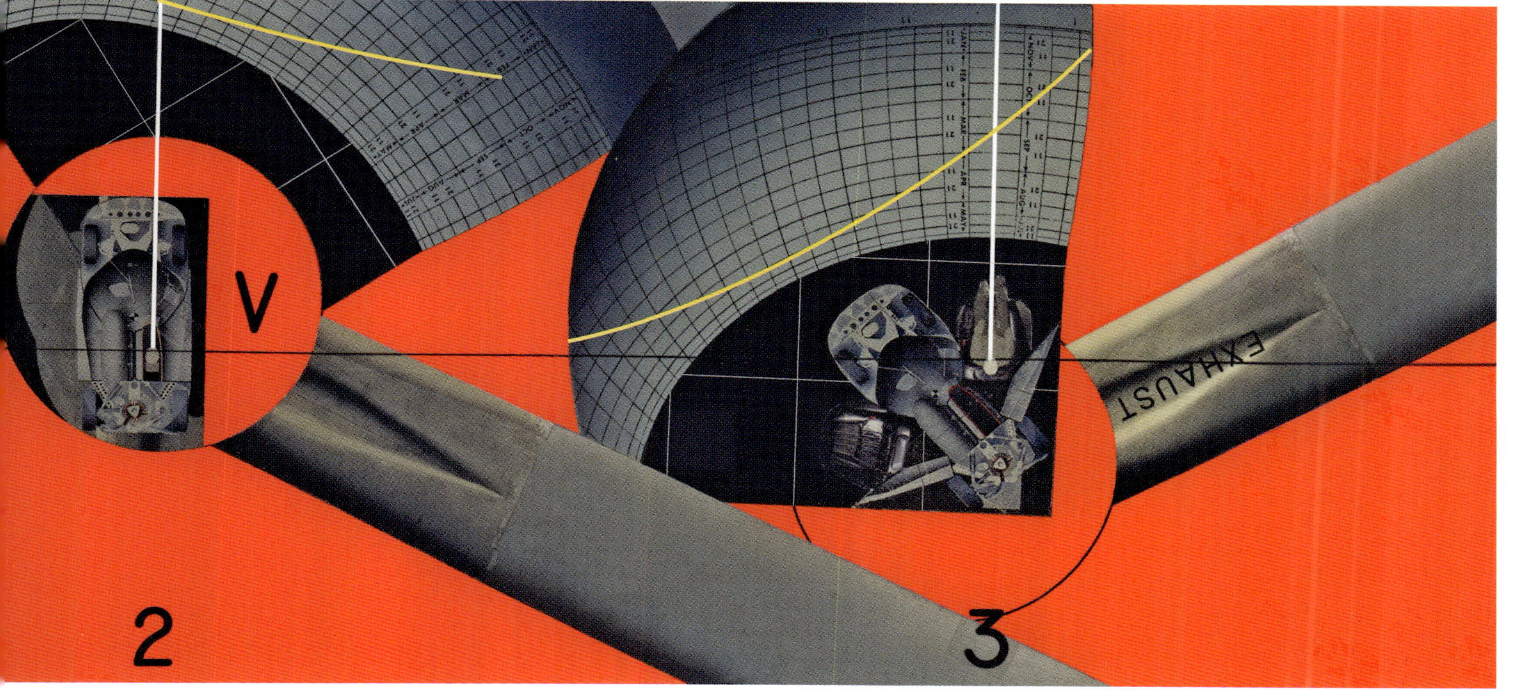

Bea Martin engages the work of Peter Cook through the motif of "blue," "a quiet anomaly of nature." She notes that the performativity and vibrancy of his city drawings find a receptive partner in the print process, with its "misregistration, vivid overlays, and material idiosyncrasies." The chromatic theme continues in Stan Allen's consideration of Smout Allen's project on rurality and the relation it sets in play between line and color, which he characterizes as "a kind of dance." The flood of color on their folio print acts, he argues, as a figure–ground amalgam that "weaves" the drawing into the page. The next article, by Adam Dayem on Shaun Murray, returns us to Morphosis, but with a difference. Murray's mode of working on layers echoes the logic of screenprinting, and he drew his own print separations, which were then exhibited as a layering of discrete sheets. These are drawings that should be experienced, Dayem argues, as "duration and as qualitative multiplicities." Following this, Jimenez Lai addresses effects of flatness and depth via Owen Nichols's desaturated reworking, in low-relief model and print, of a Michael Graves image. The effects of the dulling down of color come to the fore, present in Graves but operating through, Lai argues, a different sensibility in Nichols.

Peter Baldwin provides an intoxicating account of Neil Spiller's contribution, which takes as its reference a print by Anthony Ames. Baldwin's article ferries us downstream through Spiller's work, fully immersed in its combination of personal mythology, memory, and imagination. Writing on Arnaud Hendrickx, Bart Verschaffel observes how his generative optical analysis of a line through the plan of Venturi, Rauch & Scott Brown's Sainsbury Wing transforms an archival "document" into a "monument" that preserves architectural work in a different way to the archive. Characterizing Hendrickx's print as "quasi-iconic," he captures something of both the radiant frontality of the gold-leaf-backed print and the recalibrated diagrammatic similitude that the process produced. Anthropologist Alex Pillen sees Nat Chard as an architect who conjures levitation by the suspension of context. She is interested in the "veil" of dots screening his parallactic print, which she understands—through analogy to "indirect language"—as non-hierarchical and entertaining of a generous ambiguity. Dots arise again in the final piece, but as the point registration of surfaces captured by photogrammetric technology. In this, Iman Fayyad writes on Michael Young's diptych of prints, produced from three sources. In it she finds the obdurate physical presence of objects paradoxically asserted by the low-resolution imagery and peripheral-but-central details, such as a power outlet indexed by the scan.

Mark West,
Montréal Spring diorama,
2021

The drawing *Broiler Street* (2021) provides
the background for this diorama, the
construction of which produces a three-
dimensional realization of the drawing and
a miniature rendering of the blossoming
of roadwork that announces the arrival of
spring in the city of Montreal. This diorama
is in the permanent collection of *Ceci ne
pas un musée* in that city.

"6th box store," A83 printmaking studio,
New York,
2025

left: An open drawer in a metal flat file reveals the somewhat neatly stacked prints from the limited-edition folio *Records of the Sixth Somewhat Annual Meeting*. Visible are contributions by Peter Cook, Perry Kulper, Michael Young, Arnaud Hendrickx, Nat Chard, Shaun Murray, Mark Dorrian & Adrian Hawker, and Natalija Subotincic. Test prints by Smout Allen and CJ Lim rest on the cabinet, while handwritten labels reading "6th box store" and "cut and erased" echo the provisional, hands-on nature of the entire endeavor.

Natalija Subotincic,
Present elsewhere,
2024

below: Beginning with a photograph of an original print by Mark Robbins and Benjamin Gianni from the A83 archive, Subotincic utilized the techniques of crumplage, embossing, and light projection to alter, ground, and introduce time into the image content.

In addition to the work presented in this issue, the A83 exhibition—the curation and design of which is described in the following article by Greg Barton—included pieces by renowned Archigram founding member Michael Webb, Perry Kulper of the University of Michigan's Taubman College of Architecture and Urban Planning, and the Montreal-based Natalija Subotincic and Mark West, co-founders of *Ceci n'est pas un musée*,[6] all of whom have been constant participants in the group's events since the first meeting in 2019.

Media Negotiations

Taken together, the works presented here show a complex array of negotiations as drawings were transformed through contact with processes of print in "a drama full of inversion and reversal and blindness and uncertainty"—to return to our epigraph drawn from Jennifer L. Roberts's writing. This affected not only the drawings' material and artifactual character but also, crucially, how they were conceptualized and their graphic elements composed and redistributed. Not only did this lead to a different way of thinking about drawing, but it also staged conditions within which participants could re-find their work, although now with a difference—transformed, for example, in the objectival by-products and tests of the print process.

Finally, our hope is that this issue of Δ will stimulate further like-minded explorations. Naturally, we are eager to see how its impetus will play out in the coming work of those involved in our collaborative project; but equally we hope that it will give inspiration for future endeavors by others whom we are yet to encounter. Δ

Notes
1. Jennifer L. Roberts, *Contact: Art and the Pull of Print*, Princeton University Press (Princeton, NJ, and Oxford), 2024, p. 5.
2. Mark Dorrian, Riet Eeckhout, and Arnaud Hendrickx (eds), *Drawing Architecture: Conversations on Contemporary Practice*, Lund Humphries (London), 2022.
3. See https://centrededesign.com/drawing-conversations-autour-du-dessin/.
4. Neil Spiller (ed.), Δ *Radical Architectural Drawing*, July/August (no. 4), 2022.
5. Roberts, *Contact*, p. 16.
6. See www.notamuseum.ca.

Installation view of "The
Sixth Somewhat Annual Meeting"
exhibition, A83 gallery,
New York,
2025

The folio box of prints welcomed
visitors to A83 as both a harbinger and
a record of the generative exchanges
unfolding between the gallery and the
group of experimental architects.

Greg Barton

Spatializing "The Sixth Somewhat Annual Meeting"

Emerging from a series of conversations about drawing, "The Sixth Somewhat Annual Meeting" presented a cadre of architects refracted through an institution's collection and expertise. Facilitated by A83, the nonprofit gallery and printmaking studio in New York led by Owen Nichols and Clara Syme, the gathering served as a conduit to explore the materiality and junction of highly sophisticated drawing practices, archival activations, and fine art printmaking processes, not to mention critical camaraderie.

On view from February 14 to March 21, 2025, the display combined recent prints and drawings by 18 participants, related items from the gallery's trove, and a limited-edition box folio of prints produced by A83 on the occasion of the event. The exhibition's design—developed by architects Syme and Arnaud Hendrickx and realized with a team including Kyle Ku, Thea Yuxin Lin, Leo Abelson, Sofia Mercado, Jasper Townsend, Ji-hoo Ahn, Hsu Chia-Ching (Archie), Evan Chiang, Gabrielle Newman, and Ester Goris—aptly communicated the show's theoretical preoccupations via its fabrication, affect, and use.

Material Assemblies and Transpositions

While the folio box is wrapped in reddish-orange book cloth, graphic designer Noah Beckwith left the greyboard underneath exposed in the interior to reveal and emphasize its construction. The greyboard, reminiscent of acid-free archive boxes, in turn became a common denominator and key element of the scenography. Whether attached to suspended metal armatures or forming a table, pedestals, and shelving, it provided a unifying material support, one that deployed a consistent language and adapted per each artwork's needs. Like a chipboard study model bearing extant pencil marks, the supports registered their manufacture and asserted a provisional quality.

The armature's tectonics comprised aluminum rods, wire, and 3D-printed components to hold drawings and lighting fixtures, evoking an architect's drafting board. An adjustable system devised by Syme permitted contingencies in order to negotiate different display variables. Taken together, the assembly embodied technical-aesthetic interests expressed by many group members and subtly nodded to the ways the site and instruments of drawing inform and affect production. As a framing device, the hanging system's hardware visually receded, heightening the floating effect of the drawings on their gray mounts.

In dialogue with the drawings lining the gallery's perimeter, artifacts from A83's collection occupied a long central table. As references or prompts, these objects spanned generations and helped catalyze the group's new transpositions. Importantly, the table functioned simultaneously as a conceptual anchor and a practical gathering

Installation views of "The Sixth Somewhat Annual Meeting" exhibition, A83 gallery, New York, 2025

At the center of the space, a custom-made vitrine table displayed drawings, artifacts from the A83 archive, and process materials that informed the creation of the exhibited prints and drawings. Along the gallery walls, printed works were suspended from metal tubes and illuminated by bespoke lighting armatures, an adjustable system designed and 3D-printed specifically for the exhibition.

place for discussion and meals. What might arise when chatting or even dining with friends amidst the archive, imbibing and digesting? Outside observers were immersed in feedback loops and encouraged to eavesdrop on echoes.

The gallery's back room was devoted to the folio, titled *Records of the Sixth Somewhat Annual Meeting*. Individual plates by the participants were installed in a straightforward serial manner in the order they appear. The exhibition-in-a-box format efficiently combined storage and distribution, and allowed for indeterminate outcomes. Indeed, the *Records* harnessed many of the attributes that made the Architectural Association Folios on which they are based so influential.

Reproducibility obviously enables the wide circulation of works, yet A83 resisted the language of the copy shop. For the protagonists, the folio's unique serigraphs and Risographs— spearheaded by Nichols and Gus Crain—were not reproductions of the "originals" featured in the front area, but more so discrete translations and collaborative exercises. Moving between the two rooms unlocked comparative readings, signaling shifts in scale, medium, dimensionality, and saturation, among other aspects.

Curiouser and Curiouser
As staid, overdetermined images ricochet around siloed virtual channels, the dogged physicality and collective environment of "The Sixth Somewhat Annual Meeting"

suggested alternative avenues to iterate, broadcast, and fund experimental drawings. In probing a variety of disciplinary issues, from inherited legacies to representational regimes, the exhibition and folio both underscored the values of shared exchange and heterogeneous, investigatory approaches towards drawing to elicit new modalities and unforeseen architectures. To paraphrase comments made by contributor and group organizer Riet Eeckhout during an opening discussion at The Cooper Union, in keeping with the exhibition's process-oriented inquiry: sometimes questions are more revealing than answers. △

LONGITUDINAL SECTION
AN EXTENSION TO THE NATIONAL GALLERY
TRAFALGAR SQUARE, LONDON
VENTURI, RAUCH AND SCOTT BROWN
MARCH 1987
ROOM KEY
MEZZANINE LEVEL PLAN
AN EXTENSION TO THE NATIONAL GALLERY
TRAFALGAR SQUARE, LONDON
VENTURI, RAUCH AND SCOTT BROWN
MARCH 1987
ROOM KEY
3
4

Paddi Alice Benson

Inkscapes, Lodestones, and Wandering Boundaries

A Material Excavation of Storm-Damaged Drawings

Architectural designer and researcher **Paddi Alice Benson** investigates the contribution of Edinburgh's Metis (Mark Dorrian and Adrian Hawker) to the A83 project with their print dialogue, *Storm Gallery*. Metis began with a pile of plans produced in the design of the Sainsbury Wing of London's National Gallery by Venturi, Rauch & Scott Brown (1987–91). These images, which had been impacted by water ingress while in storage, were ready to be reworked, re-layered, re-read, and metamorphosed anew.

Venturi, Rauch & Scott Brown,
Drawings (water-damaged) of the Sainsbury Wing
at the National Gallery,
London (1987),
photographed in 2024

A sedimented pile of silkscreen transparencies from the John Nichols Printmakers & Publishers Collection held within the A83 archive in New York. They had been previously stored in John Nichols's house in Princeton, New Jersey, where they were damaged by flooding at the time of Hurricane Irene in 2011. Stained by rusty water and mold growth, and welded together by damp, the drawings were photographed by Metis at Edinburgh College of Art, University of Edinburgh, UK, in 2024.

"Storm Gallery" is the overarching title of a series of works by Mark Dorrian and Adrian Hawker, co-founders of the architectural atelier Metis. Its story begins with the invitation in 2023 to visit the A83 gallery and printmaking studio in New York in order to select an artifact from their archive and create a new work in response to it. Interested in the materiality of drawing, Metis chose a matted pile of transparencies (and related ephemera) made to produce silkscreen prints of Venturi, Rauch & Scott Brown's plans for the Sainsbury Wing of the National Gallery in London (1991). These had been damaged by flooding during the passage of Hurricane Irene in 2011, while being stored in the house of John Nichols—the print studio's founder—in Princeton, New Jersey. Ferrous water from drainage pipes spilled over the drawings, and mold developed in the intervening years. Stained and stuck together, the sedimented sheets began to print onto one another. It became clear that Metis was not engaging with a simple image of printed works but with a complex material thing marked by various adventures that had led to non-intentional forms of drawing.

As Metis set out to explore the internal topographies of the compacted pile of sheets, ideas emerged such as, the question of the archive as a "living presence"; how archival material might be reinterpreted and enlivened through ways of working upon it; possibilities of different forms of mediation in order to transform the drawing and how these might provoke kinds of spatial practice; and the status of authorship, when participants are human *and* non-human (such as weather events). The exploration of these ideas culminated in an exhibition, where *Storm Gallery* was presented as one of sixteen re-imagined works by a collective of architects for "The[ir] Sixth Somewhat Annual Meeting," hosted and presented by A83 (February 14 to March 21, 2025).

Retracing the materialization of *Storm Gallery* allows us to see some of the different ways in which the drawings were worked with and re-sedimented, becoming active agents in their own excavation. We will move from the photographing of the transparencies on a lightbox to photocopying and folding acetate prints, to the generation of topographies from strips of selected paintings held in the Sainsbury Wing, to CNC routing experiments, to the carving of oak frames and the casting of bronze objects, to a video documenting the process of separating the original artifact into layers, to, finally, the production of a new silkscreen print and a smaller-scale Risograph print for the New York exhibition.

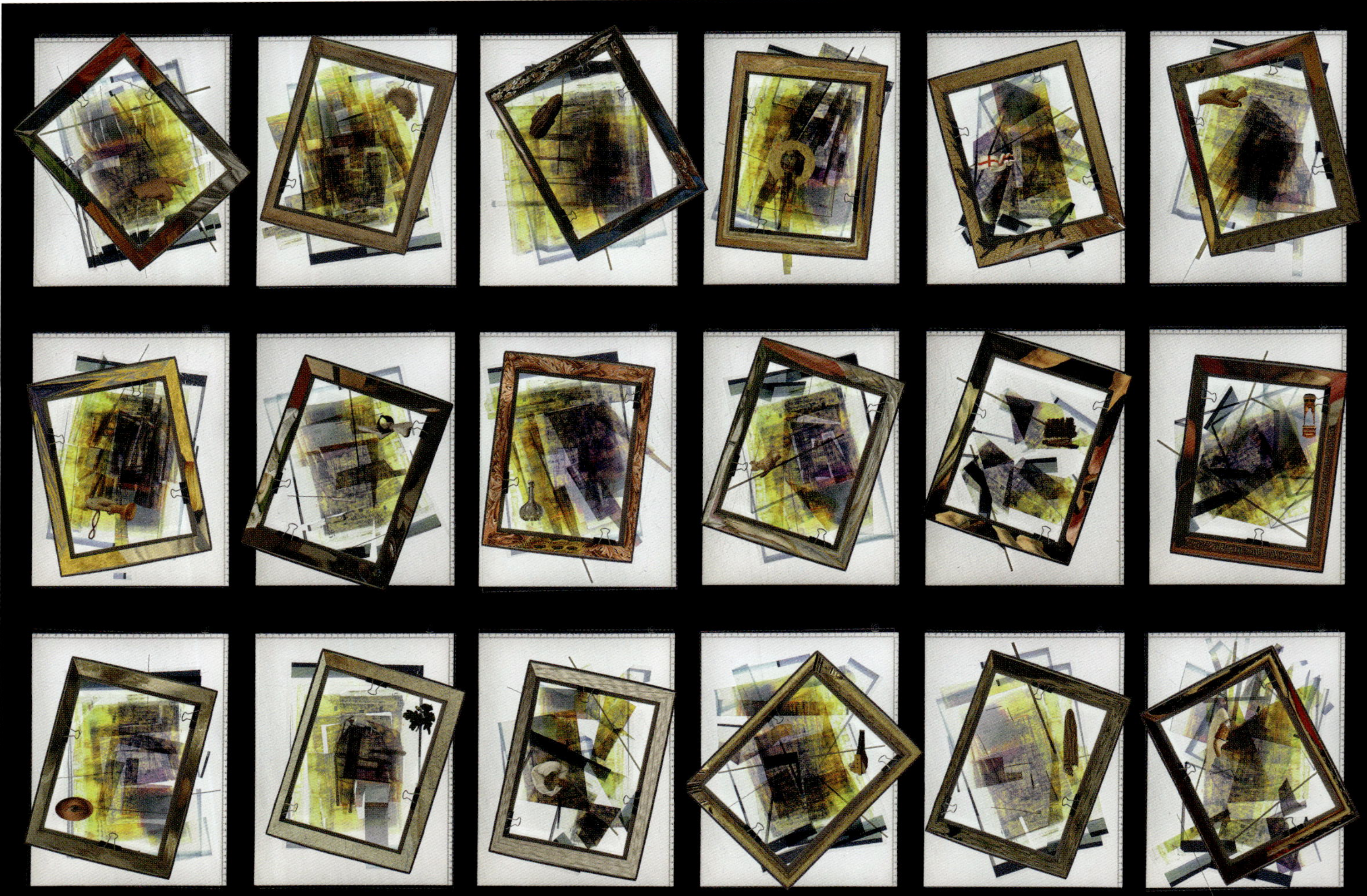

Metis: Mark Dorrian + Adrian Hawker,
Lightbox constructions,
Storm Gallery,
2024

opposite: Metis developed 18 acetate constructions to explore ways of working with the Venturi, Rauch & Scott Brown storm-damaged drawings. These corresponded to the 18 rooms of the Sainsbury Wing in the National Gallery. The excavation of the compacted image through these constructions began with scoring, cutting, and folding A4 transparency prints, in the manner of an anatomical drawing. The work was carried out on lightboxes, with the accumulated cut marks recorded.

Metis: Mark Dorrian + Adrian Hawker with Richard Collins, Digital extracts and texture mapping, *Storm Gallery*, 2024

left: A series of strips derived from a selected painting in each of the 18 rooms of the Sainsbury Wing—based on the display when the gallery opened in July 1991—were digitally processed according to their tonal values, to produce a sequence of topographies that would be applied to the internal faces of the frames. Lighter-toned areas protrude, while darker ones recede—as in the folded example floating above the array of strips here.

Sites of Emergence I:
Transparencies, Lightboxes, and a Cutting Mat

On their return from New York, Metis unrolled the original Venturi, Rauch & Scott Brown drawings and began by photographing them using a lightbox. Light filtered through in different ways. Where ferrous stains and layers of storm debris were most concentrated, the material was opaque, producing areas of dark within the photograph. In other areas, the material's transparency survived, allowing an array of lines and text from the original plan drawings to come forward. This in turn produced a vivid range of luminescent colors, moving from blackened purples to orange browns, Rubylith reds, bright yellows, faded blues, grays, and white. The constructed photograph became a compound drawing of abstracted lines, back-to-front text, and dense overlays of color, shadow, and material residue.

This image was then printed (and multiply re-printed) onto A4 sheets of acetate using a photocopy machine. The resulting transparent prints became test sites to be worked into, almost like anatomical drawings—trials with processes of scoring, folding back, peeling away, cutting open, re-folding, overlaying, and supporting, with the idea that they would be applied in due course to the original artifact. During this, a clear sheet of Perspex was used as a cutting mat, and so, when these three-dimensional constructed experiments were each re-photographed above the lightbox, they incorporated their own marks of transformation as a quiet and subtle accumulation of scored, cut, and folded lines.

In the process of printing the image onto acetate, a light blue strip appeared around the edges of the print. An accidental by-product of the process, this derived from the border of the lightbox, which left its trace as a sort of faded watermark that inadvertently recalled the flood stains of Hurricane Irene. Both the lightbox and its wandering border played an important role in the project's enfolding, which was directed by the effects of the light-filtered layers and the way that images began to bleed through one another—this, in turn, setting up a relationship with the way that the inkscape would eventually filter through the screens from which the final exhibition print was made.

Sites of Emergence II:
Paintings, Topographies, Carvings, and Castings

Venturi, Rauch & Scott Brown's project was developed to house
the National Gallery's Early Renaissance collection. When it
opened in July 1991, it displayed over 300 artworks across 18
interlinked rooms. Accordingly, 18 acetate constructions were
developed by Metis, each notionally related to one of these
spaces. Based on the catalogue of the first hanging, a painting
from each room was selected—these included Leonardo da Vinci's
Virgin of the Rocks (1491–9 and 1506–8), Antonio and Piero
del Pollaiuolo's *The Martyrdom of Saint Sebastian* (1475), and
Piero della Francesca's *Saint Michael* (1469). Next, a linear strip
was taken from each of these paintings as a digitally magnified
extract. From the painting of *Saint Michael*, for example, we see
the Archangel's red toe pressing into the scaled body of a snake,
the head of which has been severed. Using the digital extracts,
Metis—working with Richard Collins at Edinburgh College of
Art—created a series of texture mappings and modeled them
three-dimensionally to offer a new kind of topography. These
topographies were produced by extruding a range of tonal values,
based on varying shades of light and dark, within the strips. Areas
that were lightest came forward, while darker zones fell to the
back, resulting in a digitally "cultured" landscape.

Based on these, six (out of a possible series of 18) oak
frames were made as another kind of viewing device to re-
frame, and hence reread, the acetate test pieces. The making of
the frames began by CNC-routing their interior surface using

the topographies derived from the painting strips. The exterior surfaces and top edge of the frames are smooth and linear, so that it is only when we look *into* the frame, above the acetate constructions and the lightboxes on which they sit, that we see this carved interior as part of an unfolding landscape spilling out from below. Positioning the frame in this way, while leaving the complex profile of the topography readable at its lower edge, gives a sense of unlimited depth, of having taken a section cut through the very plans being looked at.

In addition to this, the frames came to support a single object extrapolated from each of the paintings and rematerialized: a copse of trees, for example, located in the far back of *The Martyrdom of Saint Sebastian* and a rock from *Virgin of the Rocks*; as well as an angel's wing, a halo, a wine flask, and an emblematic flag. These selected moments were digitally thickened, cast in bronze, and supported by steel armatures within their corresponding frames, like lodestones over discrete, self-contained weather systems or force fields of lines. Importantly, these objects were selected not for their figurative nature, nor representational value, nor significance to the painting itself, but instead because they seemed to reticently offer a new textural fragment that would weigh upon our material reading of the space they would come to inhabit.

In this way, the carved oak frames functioned at two different scales—as lightbox constructions for reading the drawings, and *as rooms themselves*. They are representatives of a continuous play of scale that takes places throughout the project—as well as through Metis's own spatial practice more generally.

This can also be seen in a diptych of linear drawing studies— the left side by Adrian Hawker (Room 4), the right by Mark Dorrian (Room 5)—that explored a different kind of response to the acetate tests. The intention behind these drawings was to work into two of the acetate experiments by re-tracing and re-interpreting their emerging architectures, while suspending their chromatic range. Here we can see a script made up of varying line thicknesses, opacity layers, neutralized tones, folded surfaces (digitally flattened), and topographic strips, as well as a textual readout from weather stations describing Hurricane Irene, which works back into the density of the original object to produce another kind of encounter.

Following their iterative studies and material experiments, Metis returned to working directly with the original drawing(s). Propelled by their initial idea of using the artifact itself to create a series of new silkscreen separations, they finally began to delaminate these sedimented drawings into four layers, each a composite able to be developed in ways trialed through the acetate studies. Extreme water damage and graphic displacement notwithstanding, in each of these transparencies we can see how the separation process in screenprinting already moves them away from more familiar forms of architectural representation in a way that harbors clear spatial potential.

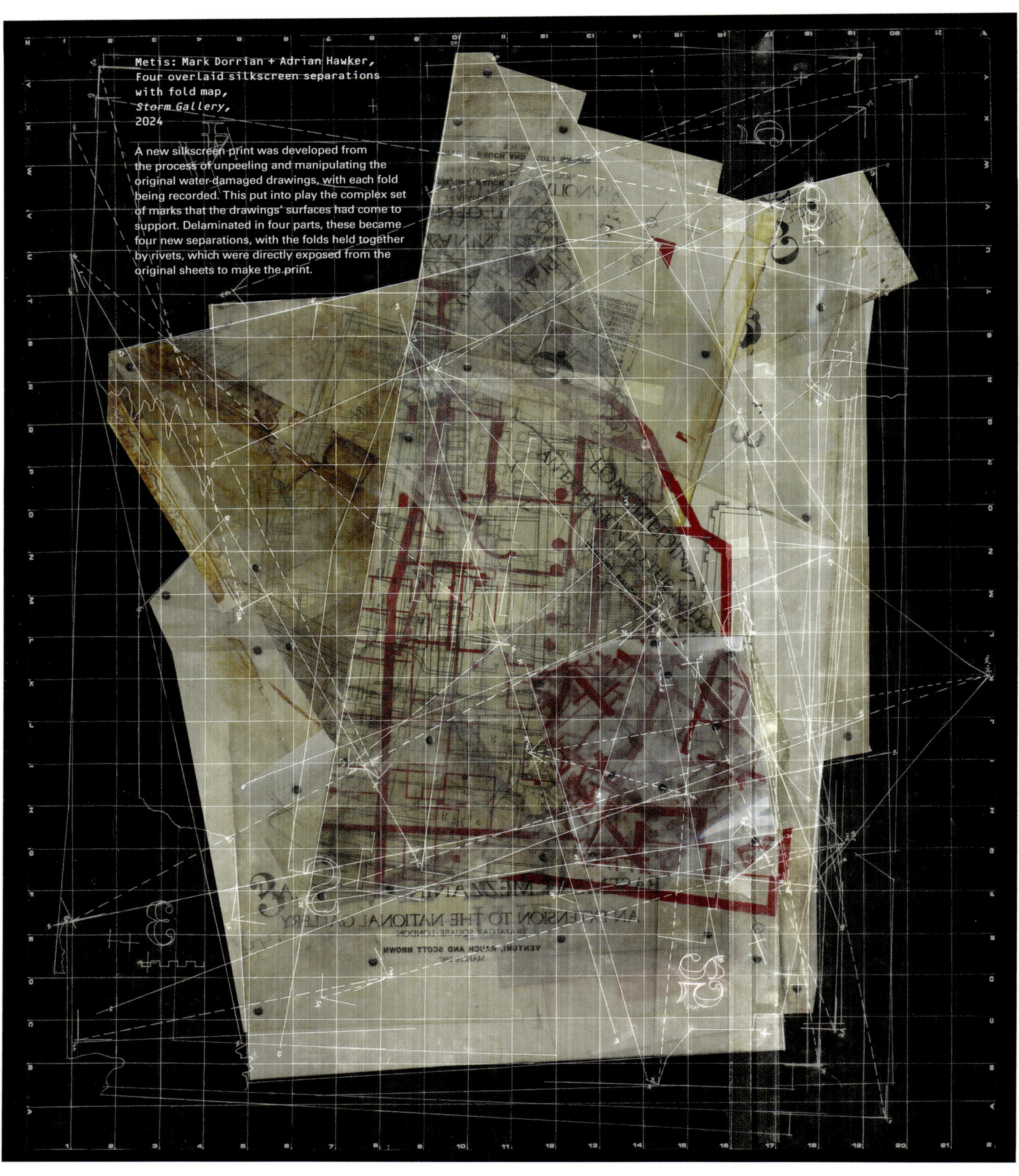

Metis: Mark Dorrian + Adrian Hawker,
Four overlaid silkscreen separations
with fold map,
Storm Gallery,
2024

A new silkscreen print was developed from
the process of unpeeling and manipulating the
original water-damaged drawings, with each fold
being recorded. This put into play the complex set
of marks that the drawings' surfaces had come to
support. Delaminated in four parts, these became
four new separations, with the folds held together
by rivets, which were directly exposed from the
original sheets to make the print.

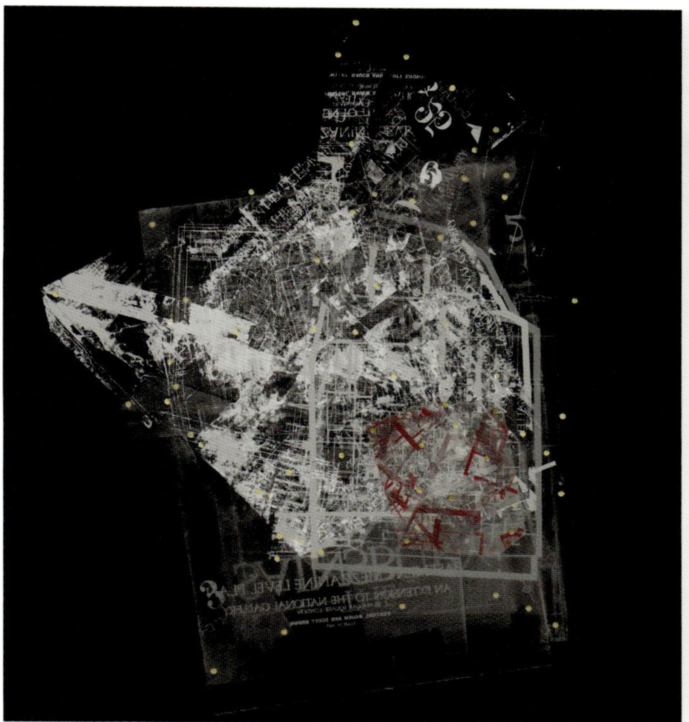

Storm Gallery:
The Sound of Drawing

A video made by Dorrian and Hawker of the delamination process
records very effectively the coming apart of the original artifact.
As they try to carefully separate its sedimented layers, we *see*
Metis getting in and among the fleecy marks of Hurricane Irene—
hands, arms, shoulders, just visible below a translucent surface
and the criss-crossing of weathered lines. And as they continue
to prize its compacted layers apart, guided by delicate areas of
resistance, we then *hear* the tension in the drawing released with a
sound like the cracking of ice. The sequence perfectly captures the
growing sense of anticipation—of not knowing how the material
will respond, or how it will transform in the process of Metis
finding their way across the surface. The video leaves unrecorded
the distinctive smell of the artifact itself …

Each of the four separations (themselves made up of between
three and eight layers) that were released from the original
mat of transparencies was developed through a series of new
folds, each marked out, cut, and fastened together using rivets.
Emboldened by this process of unpeeling and folding, Metis went
on to prepare the delaminated drawings (in their storm-damaged
state) for a new silkscreen print. It was not until "The Sixth
Somewhat Annual Meeting" however, having sent the separations
back across the Atlantic in order to be printed by A83, that their
resultant prints were seen; a large silkscreen print accompanied
by a smaller Risograph print of one the four separations. In both
cases, Hurricane Irene makes its way across their papery surface—
ending in New York, fully "(Absorbed)," to quote the closing
word of the weather readout.

An Endnote

In closing, the question of where the drawing, as both artifact
and action, begins and ends falls away, as it is replaced and
better understood by retracing how it has developed in
different situations. In this project, drawing circulated through
an array of contexts: lightboxes, oak frames, digital processing
software, a bronze forge, processes of printing, a gallery in
New York, to name but a few. In all of these, we find that
something new and unexpected comes to the surface—as
the drawing itself is mediated and transforms through these
different kinds of encounter, an active agent within this creative
and ongoing exchange. ⌀

Metis: Mark Dorrian + Adrian Hawker,
Mock-up for a new silkscreen print,
Storm Gallery,
2024

above left: Before sending the four separated sheets back to the A83
archive, Metis scanned each layer and prepared a mock-up—that included
their relative positions, order, and color—for the production of a new
silkscreen print. This was composed of three different shades of gray,
Rubylith red, and gold-leaf yellow on a black background.

Metis: Mark Dorrian + Adrian Hawker,
Storm Fold 3: a new Risograph print,
Storm Gallery,
2025

above right: As part of the *Storm Gallery* series, a smaller Risograph print
was also developed by Metis in conversation with A83. Eponymously
titled *Storm Fold 3* and printed onto vellum, it presents one of the four
delaminated drawings—the third separation and its Rubylith masking
film—accompanied by a cloud of weather data describing the passage
of Hurricane Irene. This is included in the limited-edition boxed folio of
prints produced by A83 to accompany the New York exhibition.

Jason Lee

Ghosts in the Archive
Dirty Realism and Material Memory

The Phantoms of A83, by CJ Lim, Bartlett Professor at University College London (UCL), was inspired by the A83 gallery's collection of prints, including Aldo Rossi's *Lighthouse* (1980), Frank Gehry's *Rebecca's Restaurant Placemat* (1991), and Bernard Tschumi's *Nine Houses for K-Town* (1982). Lim began with a blank, two-dimensional sheet of white paper, which he gradually transformed using a variety of both physical and narrative processes. New York architect and educator **Jason Lee** delves into Lim's methodology and graphic storytelling, exposing the ghosts within.

CJ Lim,
*The Phantoms of A83:
Misinformation Masquerading
as Truth,*
2025

One of the last iterations of the 3D-printed embossing plate developed by Owen Nichols and the team at the A83 gallery. For the form to gently press into the paper, the design of the shapes had to be carefully calibrated to avoid any damage to it.

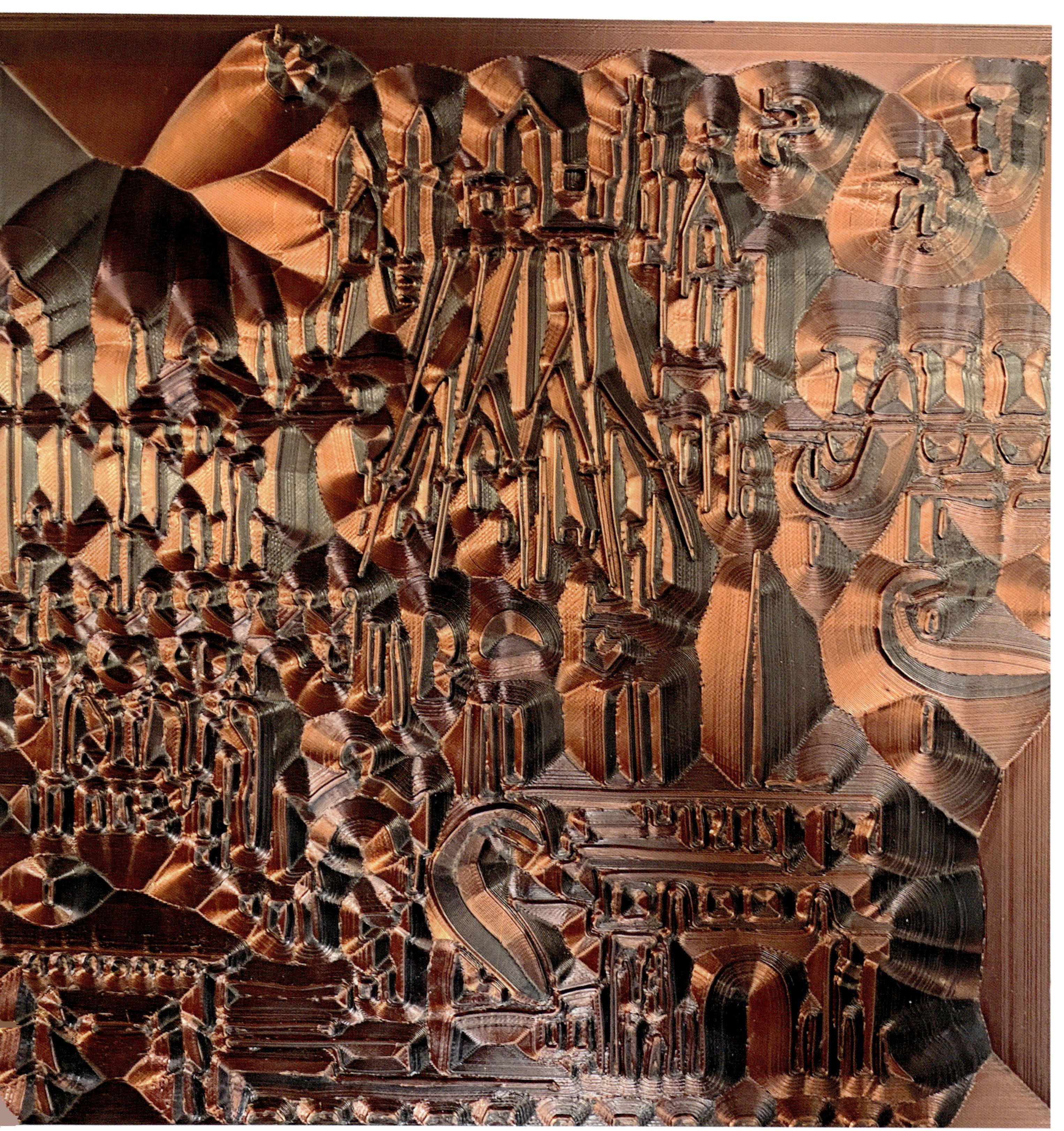

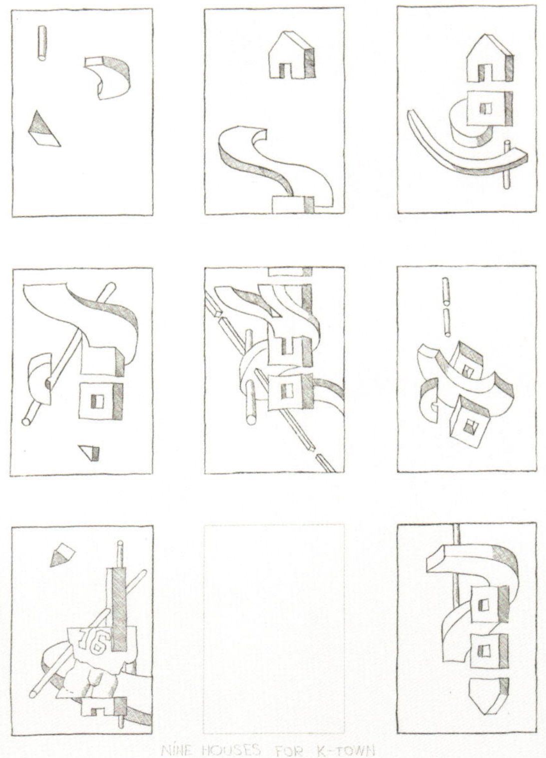

In *The Phantoms of A83*, CJ Lim assembles an architectural ghost story—not of fear, but of memory, materiality, and blurred lines between fiction and fact. Quiet yet intricate, this embossed and screenprinted work, which was part of "The Sixth Somewhat Annual Meeting" exhibition at the A83 gallery in New York, functions as both artifact and allegory. Beneath its delicately raised figures of shadows and fluorescent pigment lies a deeper narrative of postmodern redemption, disciplinary memory, and the choreographed entanglement of architectural speculation and physical production.

Activating the Archive: Fragments and Futures
The invitation to examine and reimagine the John Nichols Printmakers & Publishers Collection at A83 situated the archive as a living, generative site, a cabinet of future potentials instead of a sealed repository of past ambitions. Within the flat-file drawers are fragments and records of past provocations, technical explorations, and speculative investigations that resist closure. The misprints and test prints of architectural representation thus became maps of prior thoughts, rich with the residue of past experiments, ready to be reread and reassembled with a new agenda. Lim's response seized upon this premise, treating the archive as an active agent in the construction of narrative and material myth, a collaborator in the ongoing dialogue between memory and invention.

For Lim, the latent provocations embedded within the archive became more than historical curiosities; they served as both material and narrative catalysts, sparking a speculative reconstruction of architectural memory through acts of collage, reinterpretation, and abstraction. His engagement with the archive operates as both a personal inquiry and a broader disciplinary reflection, probing how fragments of the past can be reassembled to speak to contemporary conditions of uncertainty. This approach speaks to the cultural anxieties of our time: What becomes of architectural memory in an era of digital amnesia? As drawings dissolve into infinite digital versions, and AI-generated architectural imagery saturates our screens, the provenance of source material grows increasingly unstable. In this condition of ubiquitous uncertainty, the question of how to meaningfully instrumentalize physical archives becomes ever more urgent, not only as a means of preservation but as a tool for critical resistance and imaginative reconstruction.

Due to circumstance, Lim's encounter with the archive was doubly mediated—limited to browsing a folder of digital scans online rather than engaging with the archive directly. Yet this constraint offered an unexpectedly contemporary point of departure; as elements were first separated digitally, then reprinted, cut, and reorganized physically, new forms of interpretation emerged. Lim likened this phase of the process to the claw machine from Pixar's original *Toy Story* (1995), in which

a mechanical claw hovers over a contained world of elements, selecting fragments seemingly at random. For him, the analogy captured the playful yet deliberate act of grasping archival fragments from a dispersed field of possibilities, assembling them into new narrative configurations. Lim used the working surface like a living columbarium, a conceptual container to hold this dispersed material, a repository of memories, designed to contain fragments of the past while remaining open to future reinterpretation. The physical separation between Lim and the archive paradoxically enabled a new proximity between disparate elements, promoting juxtapositions that fostered unexpected narratives. Lim recognized a parallel between this virtual detachment and the pervasive uncertainty of contemporary information flows. Just as facts mutate across platforms, the fragments of the archive, once filtered through Lim's distant lens, became speculative figures, transformed through acts of reinterpretation, redefinition, and material manipulation.

Architectural Phantoms: Rossi, Tschumi, and Gehry
Out of this dispersed field of archival possibilities, three sources rose to the surface: Aldo Rossi's *The Lighthouse* (1981), Bernard Tschumi's *Nine Houses for K-Town* (1982), and Frank Gehry's *Rebecca's Restaurant Placemat* (1996)—each a spectral remnant of architectural memory, repurposed to navigate the speculative terrain Lim constructs.

Rossi's lighthouse, supported by tentacle-like angled foundation piles, strikes a commanding silhouette, assuming the role of a modern Noah's Ark amid a catastrophic flood of Manhattan. In Lim's reimagining, the lighthouse becomes not only a beacon but an emblem of redemption for the Postmodern movement itself.

Tschumi's *Nine Houses* recalls the sequential frames of his "Manhattan Transcripts" (1976–81),[1] where forms and spatial relationships are fragmented and reconfigured by narrative events. Lim liberates these forms by removing the bounding frames, allowing the elements to drift, float, and hover over the inundated cityscape. What began as an exercise in fragmented narrative becomes a set of fleeting angels—ephemeral, dispersed, yet retaining traces of order within dissolution.

The field of frenetic sketches interlaced over the placemat from Rebecca's, an iconic restaurant in Venice, California, completed by Frank Gehry in 1985,[2] embodies the search of new forms and shapes away from the stable composition of Modernism. Gehry's skeletal fish sketches, rendered here as a dynamic wireframe, capture the vitality of a constructed fish mid-splash. In Lim's composition, the fish navigates this reimagined terrain as both a playful and persistent figure, embodying vitality amid uncertainty.

Together, this triad forms a constellation of late 20th-century architectural anxiety. Lim suggests that the "Deconstructivist Architecture" exhibition, curated by Philip Johnson and Mark Wigley at the Museum of Modern Art (MoMA), New York, in 1988,[3] signaled the beginning of the end of the Postmodernism movement in architecture.[4] The institutional authority of MoMA, he argues, was powerful enough to overwrite existing narratives and destabilize the foundations of Postmodernism itself. In Lim's projective reconstruction of an alternative timeline of architectural movements, Rossi's lighthouse stands as the ark of salvation for Postmodernism, while Tschumi's angels and Gehry's fish drift through this transitional moment as they negotiate the currents of disciplinary flux despite their role as featured participants of the Deconstructivist exhibition.

Lim's compositional strategy echoes English architect and archaeologist Charles Robert Cockerell's *A Tribute to Sir Christopher Wren* (1842), itself an elaborate architectural collage of memory and reverence. At its center, where St. Paul's Cathedral anchors Cockerell's arrangement, Rossi's lighthouse now assumes the dominant position. Where Cockerell assembles Wren's oeuvre into a confident display of continuity, Lim submerges his fragments—including elements from Wren—within a deluged landscape, crafting an allegory for climate crisis and disciplinary transformation. Rather than disintegrate, these fragments drift and endure, spectral yet resilient, within Lim's flooded cityscape.

Material Realism: Process, Pressure, and Collaboration

The transformation from speculative collage to material artifact unfolded in close collaboration with Owen Nichols and Clara Syme, co-directors of the A83 gallery, who led the team behind the work's complex physical production. Once Lim had converted his hand-cut collages into a field of minimal abstract shapes, stripped of detail, the A83 team developed 3D-printed embossing plates, engineered to withstand the immense pressures of printmaking by increasing filament density.

The process was both iterative and tactile. The polylactic acid (PLA) filament surfaces had to be carefully smoothed, while successive plate iterations were tested and refined for depth, clarity, and structural integrity. Every parameter—drying times, ink coverage, alignment, and layering—was meticulously adjusted to achieve optimal results. This practice became a choreography of precision and improvisation. Studio notebooks—the "procedural memory" of the process—carefully recorded each adjustment, preserving practical knowledge alongside the finished artifacts.

Charles Robert Cockerell,
A Tribute to Sir Christopher Wren,
1842

opposite: Lim used Cockerell's architectural drawing as a conceptual composition organizer; note Cockerell's placement of London's St Paul's Cathedral as the central anchor.

CJ Lim,
The Phantoms of A83: Living Columbarium,
2025

below: Lim's initial container of building parts as inspired by the claw machine in Pixar's *Toy Story* (1995) and the field of parts from Christopher Wren's UK portfolio.

Such procedural memory underscores the significance of A83 as not only an archive of prints, but an archive of practice itself. Nichols notes how few projects ever repeat the same workflow; each is uniquely negotiated, and the tools of production—jigs, plates, ink mixtures—become control points as valuable as the final prints.[5] These works record not perfection, but the realities of making: the moments of improvisation that define the craft.

Rather than sanitize imperfection, Lim and Nichols embraced the nuanced personalities of the prints. The depth of the embossing, the fibrous textures, and the spectral glow of fluorescent ink can all be read through the lens of "Dirty Realism" coined by the American author and journalist Bill Buford in 1983 to describe a group of North American writers "devoted to the local details, nuances, the little disturbances in language and gesture."[6] This sensibility resonates with the attention devoted to unassuming details: the precise plate geometry, calibrated pressure, and layered felt padding, all orchestrated to produce just enough material stretch to create the raised figure and cast a soft shadow.

Retired Canadian Professor of Architectural History and Theory Liane Lefaivre adopts Buford's premise and extends it beyond literature, proposing that the sensation of perception can be more significant than knowing. Such perception promotes defamiliarization, transmitting new meanings and values through the ordinary.[7] Lim's *Phantoms of A83* captures this spirit: every press mark, shadowed groove, and procedural misalignment becomes a record of making.

Spanish architect and Professor of Architecture Jesús Vassallo's reflections in *Seamless: Digital Collage and Dirty Realism in Contemporary Architecture* (2016) further transpose this thinking into the digital realm, where the erasure of visible seams produces a new kind of realism.[8] Although focused on digital collage, Vassallo's insights resonate with Lim and Nichols's process. Their transatlantic collaboration—unfolding across digital sketches, physical prints, and layered inks—exemplifies the entangled realities of production today, where the line between digital precision and material imperfection is deliberately blurred. In *The Phantoms of A83*, the incremental removal of seams and edges transforms the work into a constructed reality: one that acknowledges its processes even as it aspires to visual continuity.

Fact and Misinformation: Plate Versus Print

One of the most compelling metaphors embedded in *The Phantoms of A83* is the ambiguous relationship between plate and print. Lim describes this duality as an allegory for fact and misinformation: is the plate a source of truth, or a tool of distortion? The plate, rigid and precise, bears the marks of intention and craft. The print, by contrast, receives this impression but carries its own autonomy—layered inks, atmospheric shadows, and a phosphorescent glow that transforms the narrative under changing conditions of light.

This ambiguity extends beyond the disciplinary frame. We inhabit an era defined by misinformation, viral falsehoods, and algorithmically amplified noise. Architectural representation, like media culture, is saturated with seductive, high-resolution renders and speculative fictions masquerading as fact. *The Phantoms of A83* acknowledges this condition, using the physical reality of embossing to project alternative narratives shaped by the viewer's perception of authenticity.

In Lim's narrative, Rossi's lighthouse, Gehry's fish, and Tschumi's angels drift not as antagonists but as cohabitants of a fluid urban ecology. They become phantoms of disciplinary memory—ghosted remnants of architectural ambitions, reshuffled and submerged yet persisting within the currents of architectural thought.

Archive, Workshop, and Gallery

Integral to this reconciliation is Lim's deliberate tribute to A83 itself. The gallery is not only an exhibitor but an active agent in architectural culture, a place where archival fragments are not merely preserved but reactivated. A83 operates as gallery, workshop, and archive: a site where disciplinary memory and future projections coalesce. In this layered role, it becomes both custodian of history and producer of new architectural imaginaries.

At a moment when architectural representation risks dematerialization in the flood of digital images and instant circulation, A83 reasserts the value of material process. It embodies civitas in its broadest sense: a space of collective engagement, procedural memory, and shared speculation. Much like the physical notebook pages Nichols's team uses to track production variables, A83 records the artifacts of architectural making, not as pristine objects, but as imprints of thought and touch, a testament to the continuing urgency of material practice in architecture's digital age.

The Phantoms of A83 ultimately serves as both artifact and provocation. It reminds us that the power of representation lies not in claims to certainty, but in its capacity to hold ambiguity— to tell stories that resist neat resolution, and to produce objects that record process as much as intention. In the tension between plate and print, fact and fiction, Lim and A83 offer not closure but invitation: an architecture of ghosts, poised between memory and projection, that invites reflection, provokes uncertainty, and inspires new disciplinary imaginaries. ᴥ

Notes
1. Bernard Tschumi, *The Manhattan Transcripts*, Academy Editions (London), 1981.
2. Paul Goldberger, *Frank Gehry: Fish Lamps*, Gagosian (New York), 2014.
3. See Philip Johnson and Mark Wigley, *Deconstructivist Architecture*, exh. cat., Museum of Modern Art/Little Brown and Co. (New York), 1988: https://assets.moma.org/documents/moma_catalogue_1813_300062863.pdf.
4. Interview with the author, April 2025.
5. Interview with the author, April 2025.
6. Bill Buford, "Editorial," *Granta*, 8, Summer 1983, p. 4.
7. Liane Lefaivre, "Dirty Realism in European Architecture Today: Making the Stone Stony," *Design Book Review*, 17, Winter 1989, pp. 17–20.
8. Jesús Vassallo, *Seamless: Digital Collage and Dirty Realism in Contemporary Architecture*, Park Books (Zurich), 2016.

ORGANIZATIONAL SYSTEMS

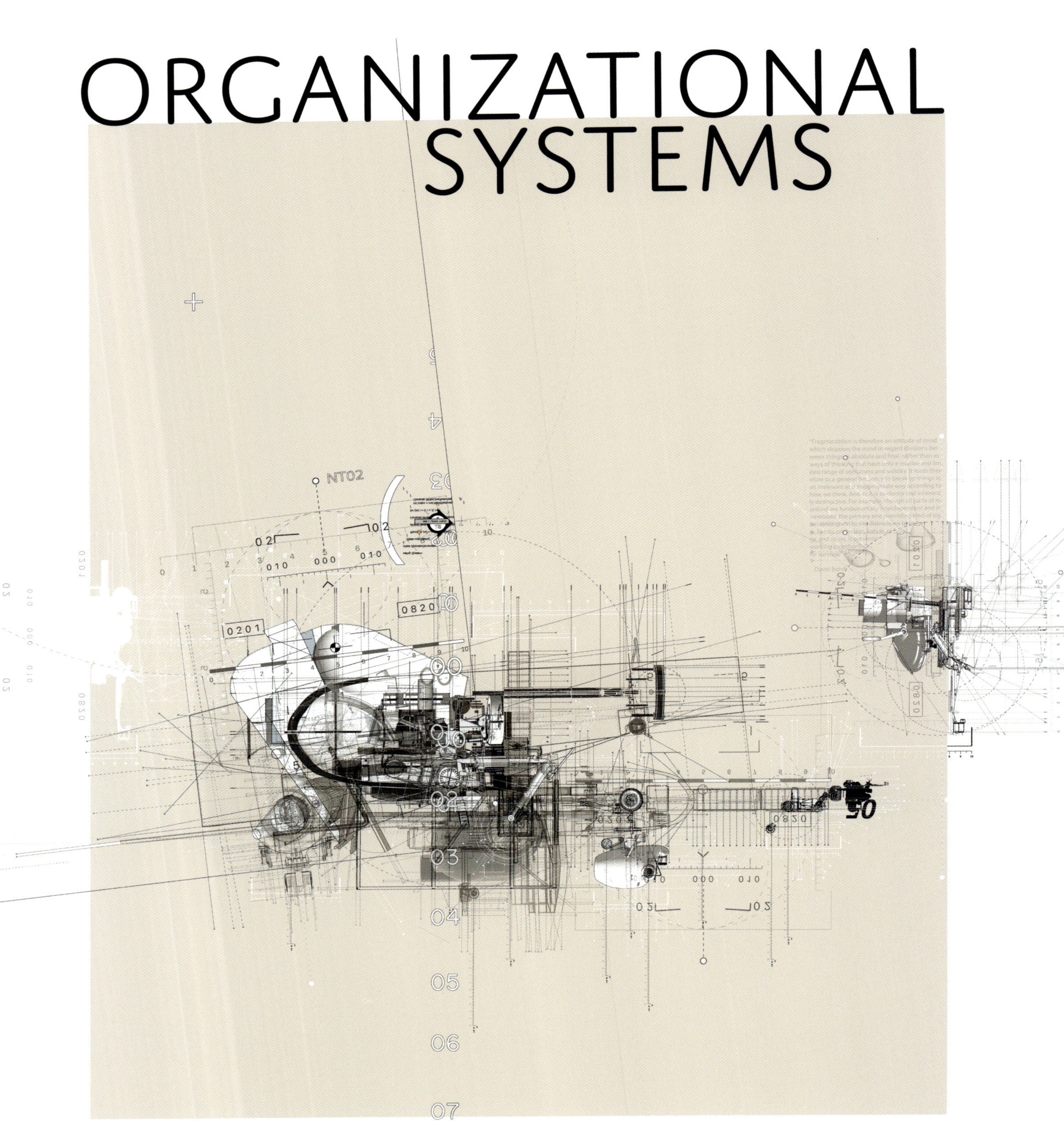

Thom Mayne

AND SPECULATIVE CONDITIONS

DRAWING AS A SITE OF INQUIRY

Bryan Cantley,
6TH ST. Artifact 11,
2024

above: Part of an expanding series of genetic splicing of post-drawing residuum onto Mayne's original print. This explores issues of the nature, typology, and structure of the *sectional poché* as a place of rebirth and cyborg operations. A new drawing typology begins to emerge with event horizon protocols.

Bryan Cantley,
New Typology Specimen 08,
2024

opposite: A diagram exploring residual space, annotative plots, and situational distortion as conditions for drawing typologies, generating new species of occupancy and interaction. Allegorical political boundaries are formed, tested, and then recalibrated to arrive at mechanisms of inquisitive manifestations.

LOS ANGELES-BASED ARCHITECT **THOM MAYNE** WRITES ON THE WORK OF ARCHITECT AND EDUCATOR BRYAN CANTLEY, WHICH REIMAGINES MAYNE'S OWN ICONIC ABSTRACTED PRINTS DEPICTING HIS 6TH STREET RESIDENCE PROJECT. HE MUSES ON CANTLEY'S INSPIRATIONS AND AMBITIONS FOR CREATING DRAWINGS THAT ARE EVEN FURTHER DISTANCED FROM THEIR 1988 SOURCE. THIS HE SEES AS A WAY TO LIBERATE THEIR CREATIVE POSSIBILITIES BEYOND THE EXPEDIENCIES AND PRAGMATICS OF CONSTRUCTION. MAYNE ATTEMPTS TO UNRAVEL THE POTENTIALITIES OF THE ARCHITECTURAL DRAWING.

Thom Mayne,
6th Street Residence,
Santa Monica, California,
1987–92

The 6th Street Residence's conceptual genesis lay in the idea of salvaging industrial artifacts and urban debris. It was a threshold project in every respect, pursuing the idea of tension in and through its non-contiguous façades.

Bryan Cantley's choice of prompt for his contributions to "The Sixth Somewhat Annual Meeting" at New York's A83 gallery in 2025 centered on a silkscreen print of the 6th Street Residence in Santa Monica, California (1987–92). The print offered more than a representation—it operated. It constructed an architectural reality, not through depiction but through the internal logic of its drawing. That became the departure for Cantley's inquiry. The composition incorporates 11 machinic found objects— each extracted from its original context and implanted into the architecture as active fragments. Importantly, the image resists static documentation; instead, it constructs a spatial and relational system within the field of the drawing itself. For Cantley, this disjunction between the built object and the organizational field suggests that fixed data in architectural drawing can disengage from the constraints of built space. His investigation initiates a broader inquiry—one that situates architectural media as autonomous, generative, and capable of activating the latent potential embedded in its residual forms.

As we see from Cantley's approach to the print, he is interested in the potential of drawing to go beyond the representation of architecture and instead to itself become it. His work rejects

the dogma of the built object as architecture's final expression, instead positioning the drawing as an autonomous force—a space of active, generative interrogation, where architecture is formed, undone, and re-formed. This is not about representation; it is about organization, structure, and provocation. A system that exists in motion, constantly evolving, resisting static resolution.

The Orthographic Tradition

Operating within—and against—the orthographic tradition, Cantley engages the drawing not as a tool of precision, but as a field of tension. A charged surface where architecture discards its conventional role as a precursor to building and reclaims itself as a space of inquiry. Drawing is not passive—it is an event, a rupture. It is a site of negotiation, where spatial and conceptual ideas collide, mutate, and reconfigure. Cantley's drawings dismantle the linear hierarchy of architectural production— drawing is not a precursor to construction but a field of investigation in its own right. Through this active process, his work creates an evolving network of relationships, reframing drawing not simply as representation, but as a speculative and epistemic operation.

The term "orthographic tradition" can be examined through the lens of French philosopher Bernard Stiegler's concept of the "orthographic age," which extends beyond conventional notions of writing and notation to encompass broader systems of technical inscription and transmission of knowledge. In *Technics and Time, 2: Disorientation* (2008; first published in French in 1994), Stiegler argues that orthography is not merely a method of representation but a technological condition of thought, shaping how knowledge is externalized, recorded, and inherited across generations.[1] The orthographic age thus marks the transition from purely oral transmission to systems of technical memory, where knowledge is inscribed through writing, images, and other symbolic forms. For Stiegler, orthography is a prosthetic form of memory, enabling the accumulation and refinement of technical knowledge over time. Architecture, like philosophy and science, has long operated within this orthographic paradigm, where drawing functions as an instrument of inscription, structuring the technical, conceptual, and material foundations of architectural production. This perspective positions architectural drawing not as a neutral representational tool but as an active epistemic device, shaping both architectural discourse and practice.

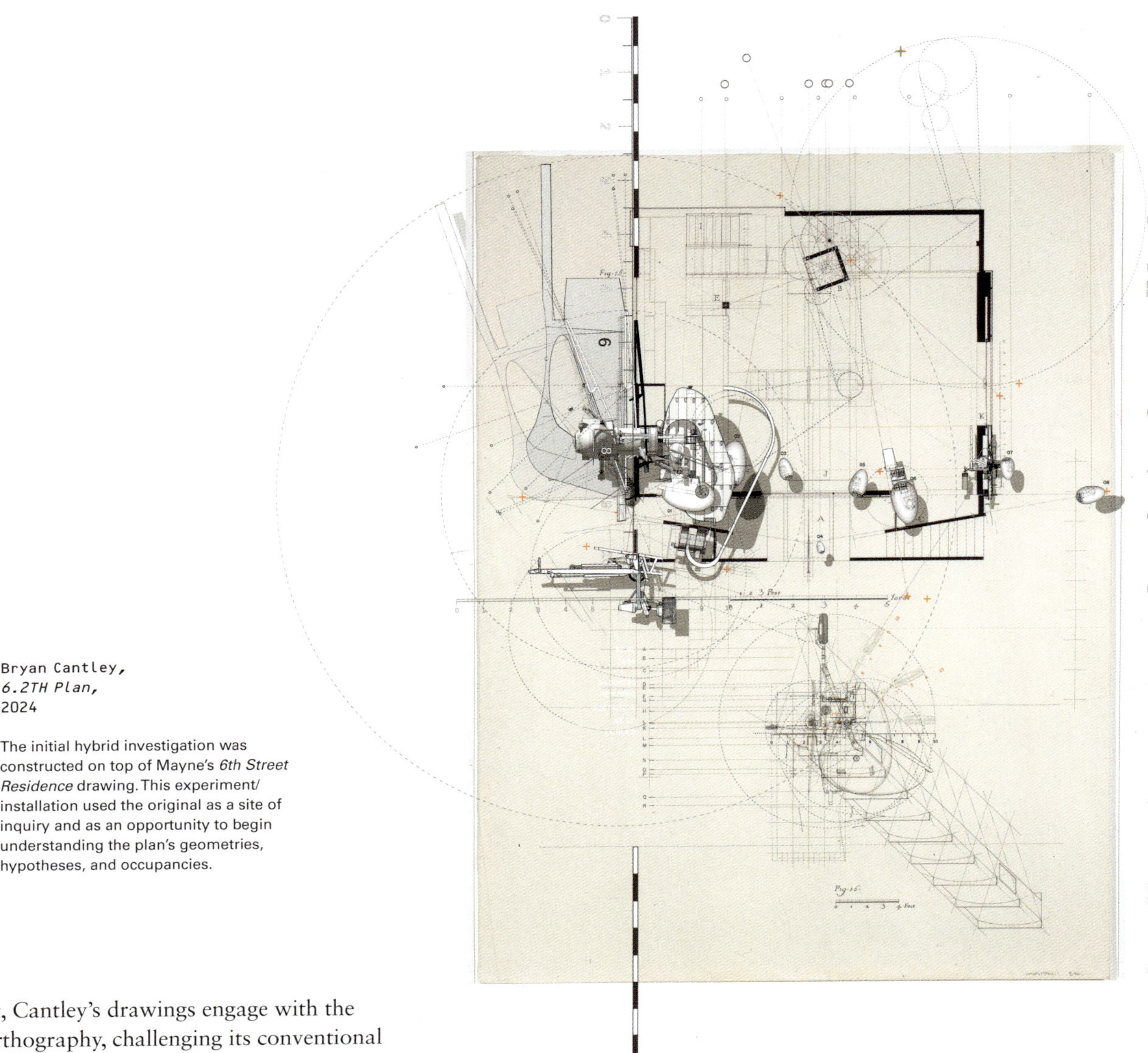

The initial hybrid investigation was constructed on top of Mayne's *6th Street Residence* drawing. This experiment/installation used the original as a site of inquiry and as an opportunity to begin understanding the plan's geometries, hypotheses, and occupancies.

Within this context, Cantley's drawings engage with the expanded notion of orthography, challenging its conventional subservience to built form. Rather than serving as a technical blueprint for construction, these drawings operate as a site of inquiry, generating architectural meaning through inscription and iteration. Their engagement with juxtaposed scales, oblique projections, and non-prescriptive compositions further complicates their relation to traditional orthographic conventions, resisting fixed interpretations and embracing open-ended spatial and conceptual possibilities. Cantley's drawings generated from the 6th Street project extend Stiegler's idea of the orthographic age, demonstrating how architectural drawing can function not just as a medium of technical transmission but as a transformative and speculative act of thinking through space, form, and structure.

The Logic of *Non-finito*

There is no singular logic in Cantley's drawings—only friction, contradiction, and dissonance. Each component, each fragment, resists fixed meaning. Orthographic precision meets non-linearity; the system resists closure. In this way, the work channels the logic of *non-finito*—not as absence, but as provocation. Incompleteness becomes a strategy for continuous becoming, allowing architectural ideas to remain in a state of active organization. Reacting to the collapsing plans, elevations, and details of the 6th Street drawings through oblique projections, distortions, and scalar shifts, Cantley's drawings interrogate the limits of coherence itself. They refuse traditional stability, opting instead for an organizational framework that is always in flux.

The concept of "*non-finito*" originates from the Renaissance sculptural technique, notably exemplified in Michelangelo's works (such as the four sculptures known as the *Prisoners* or *Slaves*, c. 1519–34, held at the Galleria dell'Accademia in Florence), where unfinished forms evoke a sense of perpetual becoming rather than a fixed finality. In the context of architecture and drawing, *non-finito* extends beyond an aesthetic choice; it signifies an open-ended process that resists resolution, embracing incompleteness as an inherent condition of creative exploration. Cantley's drawings embody this *non-finito* philosophy, treating the unfinished as a fundamental architectural strategy rather than a lack of completion. His drawings resist fixed interpretations, engaging with multiple meanings and evolving associations. This aligns with architectural discourse that sees the unfinished not as failure but as potential, allowing the work to remain in flux, adaptable, and generative over time. Such an approach positions drawing and architectural speculation as continuous acts, where process supersedes product, and the work remains perpetually in dialogue with its interpretations.

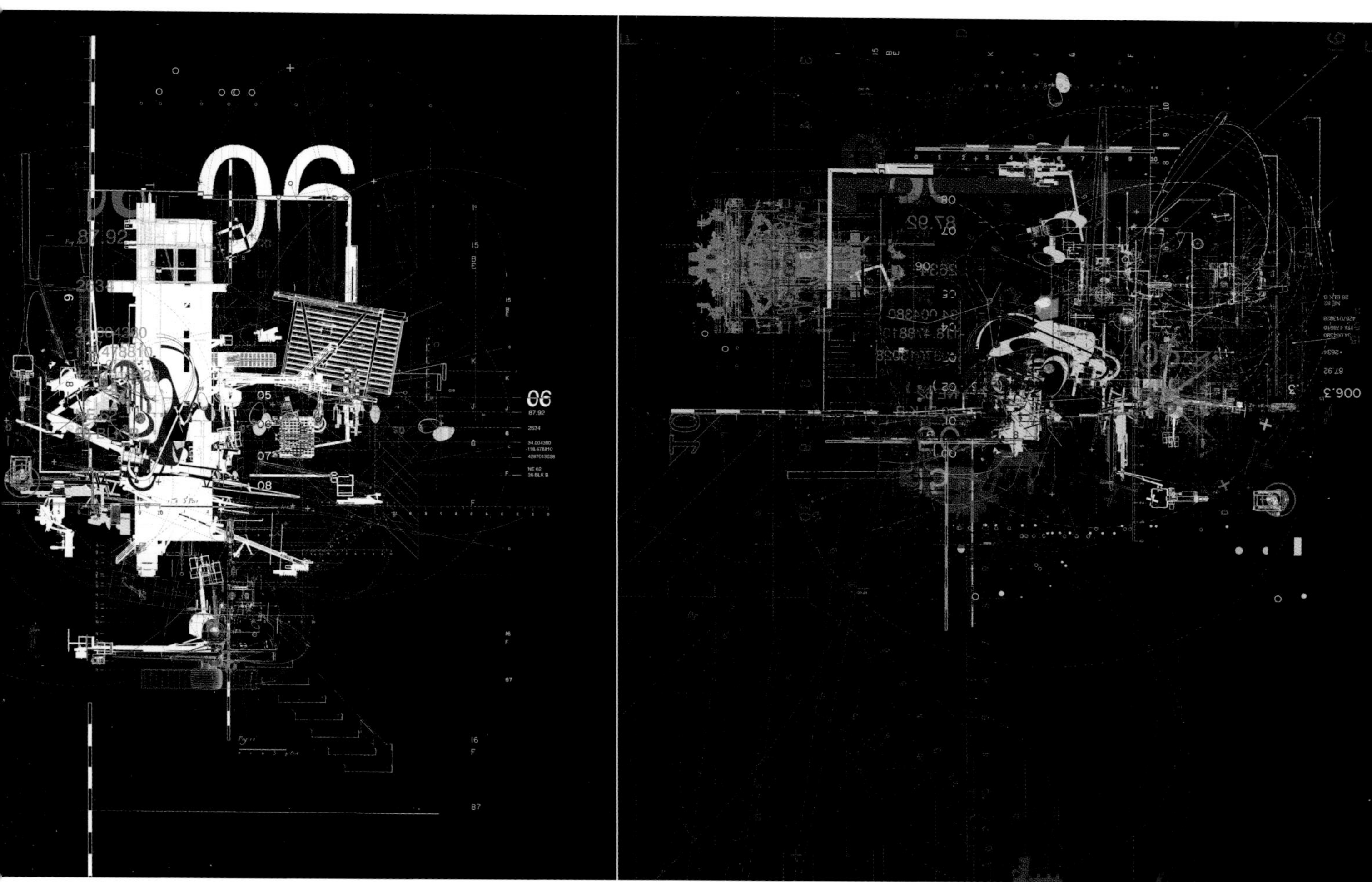

Dead Tech

Cantley's drawings exist at the intersection of technology and obsolescence. The mechanical elements from the 6th Street drawings, severed from their functional past, are reinterpreted as autonomous systems. These aren't machines of efficiency; they are machines of disruption—objects that exist between categories, defying typology. Here, the machine is no longer a tool of production but a medium of conceptual reconfiguration, an ephemeral and romantic object, much like the dead technologies of the industrial past. This is the core of "Dead Tech"—the machine not as a device but as a relic, an entity that outlives its purpose and assumes new spatial roles. Materiality is no longer dictated by function—it is unfixed, reactivated, and embedded within a new associative system.

Bryan Cantley,
6TH ST. Residues 04/05,
2024

These first experiments used the residual spaces, notations, and assemblies from the initial installation drawings as fodder for new spatially responsive prototyping. This is the beginning of the act of erasure of the original print artifacts, in pursuit of an autonomous drawing condition and genus.

In *Dead Tech: A Guide to the Archeology of Tomorrow* (1981), Manfred Hamm and Rolf Steinberg explore the remnants of obsolete industrial and technological artifacts, capturing their decay and transformation into relics of a past industrial vision.[2] The book serves as a photographic and conceptual study of abandoned machines, defunct infrastructure, and technological obsolescence. Rather than viewing these machines solely as functional instruments, *Dead Tech* reframes them as ephemeral and romantic artifacts, embodying both nostalgia and the transient nature of technology. The photographic documentation presented in the book emphasizes the atmospheric and melancholic beauty of these decaying forms, situating them within a broader historical and cultural context that acknowledges their once-vital role in shaping industrial society. By treating these mechanical remains as aesthetic and conceptual objects, *Dead Tech* invites a reflection on the life cycle of technological systems—their birth, utility, abandonment, and eventual reabsorption into the landscape. The images often highlight the corrosion, fragmentation, and partial disintegration of these machines, underscoring the inevitability of obsolescence and the shifting values assigned to technological artifacts over time. In this light, the book functions not only as a record of decline but as an active critique of progress narratives that prioritize innovation without accounting for material afterlives.

This perspective aligns with the reinterpretation of mechanical elements in Cantley's drawings, where function is displaced in favor of material presence, associative meaning, and evolving organizational relationships. Just as *Dead Tech* challenges viewers to see technological detritus as sites of potential meaning, Cantley's architectural work reactivates obsolete or ambiguous elements, placing them within speculative frameworks that resist instrumental closure. In both cases, what was once utilitarian becomes conceptual, and the obsolete becomes a ground for new architectural and intellectual possibilities.

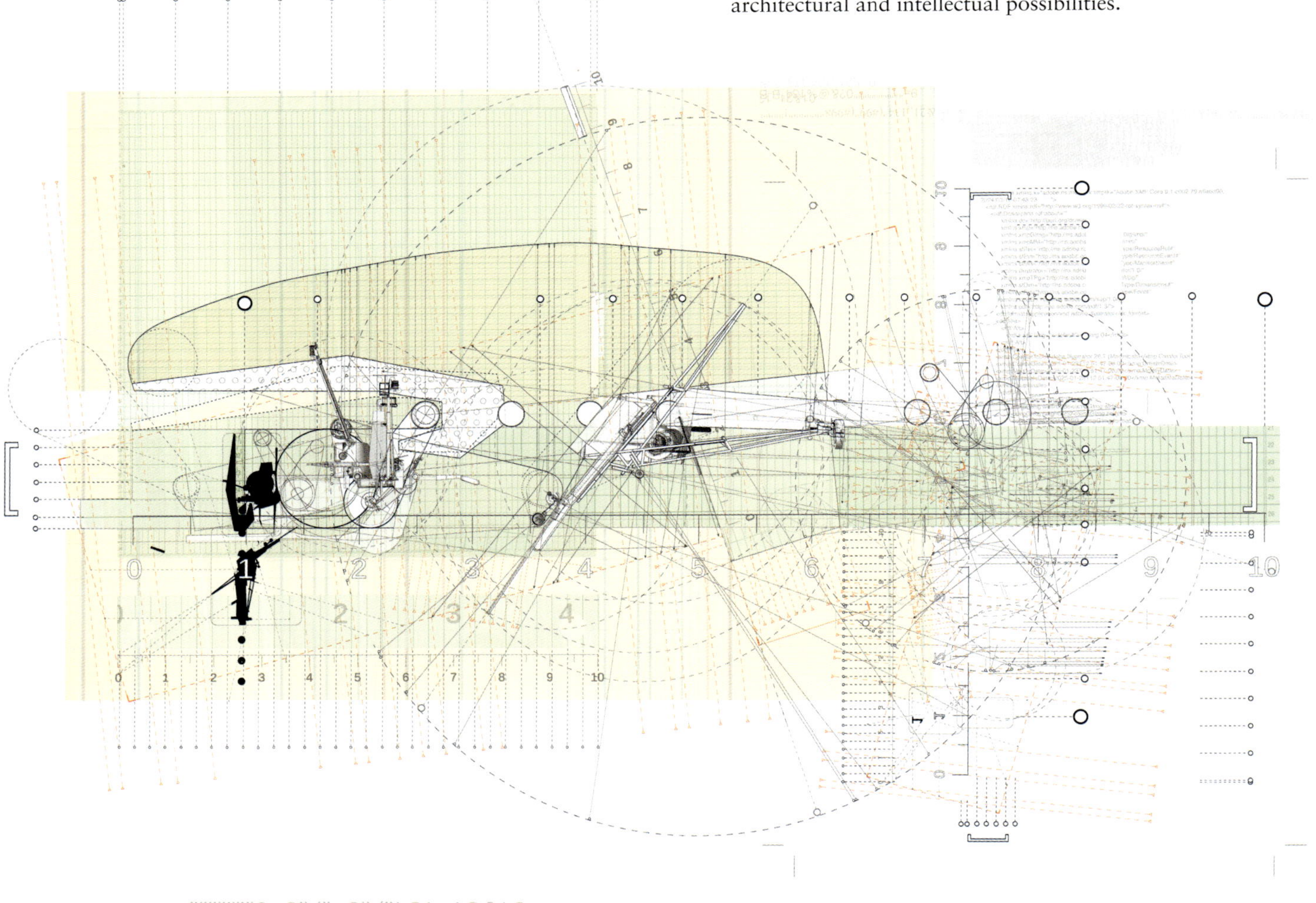

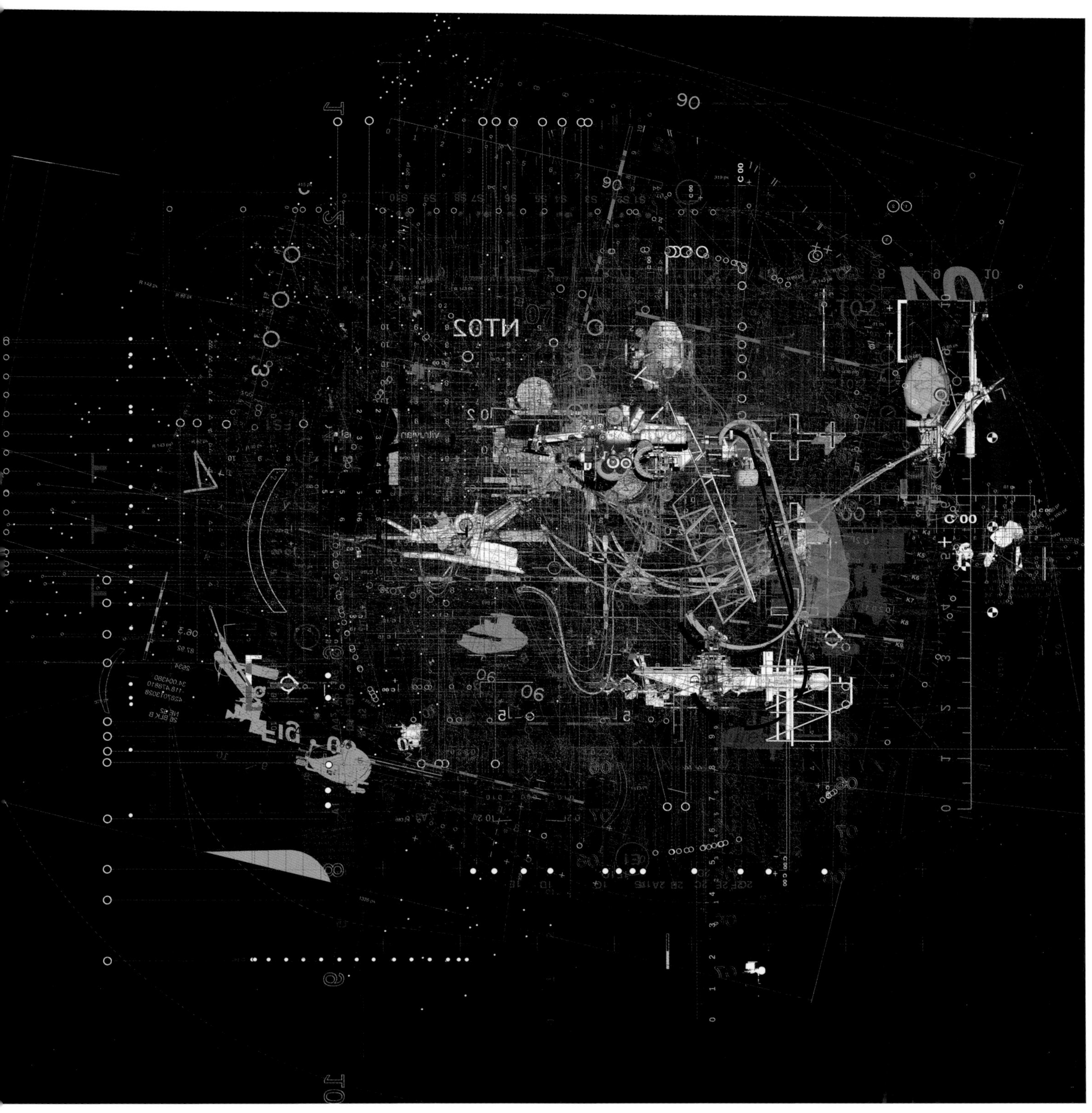

Bryan Cantley,
Cyborg Datascape 04,
2024

opposite: An offspring of a series of a
new investigative species—exploring
the harvesting of notational fields,
annotative spaces, and data sets
as equivalent participants in
dimensional, compositional, and
tactical dialogues.

Bryan Cantley,
Data 09-G,
2024

above: Expansion of the residual-
space cosmos. Annotations become
as equally governing as their formal
counterparts. The space between the
entity, its backdrop, its focal point,
and its context is destroyed and
reformulated. Conventional roles
of fore-, mid-, and backgrounds are
alchemically distorted.

FREED FROM THEIR ORIGINAL UTILITY, THESE ELEMENTS
FORM A NON-LINEAR NETWORK, GENERATING SHIFTING
SPATIAL AND ORGANIZATIONAL RELATIONSHIPS

Bryan Cantley,
Cyborg Datascape 08,
2024

Evolution of what Cantley terms the
"n'object" (the non-object). Spatial
definitions, historical contexts, and relational
classifications are abolished, in pursuit of an
unprecedented taxology. This is the space
where coherence with traditional rules of
segregation, definition, and autonomy is
disqualified and reinvented. Data and objects
converge to form a new line of aggregated
spatial inquiries.

Part–Whole Relationships

Freed from their original utility, these elements form a non-linear network, generating shifting spatial and organizational relationships. Part–whole relationships are obliterated—nothing exists in singularity, only in dynamic interaction. This is not composition; it is collision—an architecture of tensions, intersections, and unresolved systems.

The part–whole relationship in architecture refers to the dynamic interplay between individual components and the larger system they compose. Traditionally, architectural theory has emphasized hierarchical unity, where parts function subserviently to an overarching whole. This approach is rooted in classical composition, as seen in Vitruvian principles and later reinforced in Modernist rationalism. However, contemporary architectural discourse—particularly Deconstructivist, parametric, and non-hierarchical systems thinking—has challenged this fixed order by promoting emergent, decentralized, and associative relationships among elements. In Cantley's drawings, part–whole relationships are destabilized—the mechanical elements do not belong to a singular totality but rather exist within a shifting field of associations. This echoes Gilles Deleuze and Félix Guattari's concept of assemblage, where components are not defined by their belonging to a whole but by their capacity to form new relationships.[3] By resisting a fixed, prescriptive composition, Cantley's drawings operate as an evolving system, where parts continuously redefine and reconfigure their spatial and conceptual roles.

The 6th Street screenprint becomes a departure for Cantley's drawings. His drawings begin with the 6th Street framework, then dismantle it. What starts as a structured engagement dissolves into an iterative exploration. Cantley's process is excavation, fragmentation, and reassembly. The technical and mechanical elements, once tied to architectural function, become pure annotation. Plans, sections, and diagrams are extracted, recombined, and placed in dialectical opposition—rejecting the certainty of prescriptive intentionality.

Spatial Manifesto-Oeuvres

Cantley's later iterations leave the 6th Street project behind, pushing into a new architectural language. He builds an autonomous system of inquiry—a space where annotations expand, mutate, and self-proliferate. Data is no longer referential but self-generating. His drawings are no longer depictions of architecture, but constructs of information, loops of spatial metadata, embedding complex organizational logics within themselves. Like Lewis Mumford's machine—no longer efficient but adaptive—Cantley's systems shift from instrument to idea, from object to operation.

In *Technics and Civilization* (1934), Mumford, the American historian and theorist of technology, architecture, and urbanism, explores the evolution of technology as an organic and adaptive force, rather than merely a system of mechanical efficiency.[4] He critiques the machine age's rigid determinism, arguing that as technology advances, it moves beyond strict mechanization and begins to mirror biological and organic processes. He suggests that technological development does not follow a linear trajectory toward efficiency but instead adapts, integrates, and becomes increasingly complex—blurring the boundaries between the mechanical and the organic. This notion resonates with Cantley's work, where machines and technical elements are no longer fixed objects of function but dynamic, evolving entities. Rather than serving as prescriptive tools, they become operative sites for reinterpretation, transformation, and speculative exploration—echoing Mumford's idea that technology should be understood as a cultural and intellectual extension rather than a mere instrument of production.

Eventually, Cantley's work is unrecognizable from its origins. What began as a recalibration of the 6th Street system becomes a new site for investigation. He terms them "spatial manifesto-oeuvres"—synthetic offspring of variational structures, where architectural systems are no longer fixed, but always contingent, always adaptive. This is where technology turns inward, where the machine is no longer an object but a condition, a medium of perpetual reconfiguration.

Departing from the 6th Street drawings' organizational idea, Cantley expands it intentionally, treating drawing not as a static representation but as a continuously evolving system. His work asserts that architecture is not an object—it is an inquiry, a space where precision and ambiguity coexist, where the boundaries between machine, body, and information collapse into an open-ended architectural order. His drawings are not illustrations of architecture but architectural conditions themselves, existing in a perpetual state of flux, continuously redefining their own possibilities. ⟂

Notes
1. Bernard Stiegler, *Technics and Time, 2: Disorientation* [1994], Stanford University Press (Stanford), 2008, pp. 15–20.
2. Manfred Hamm and Rolf Steinberg, *Dead Tech: A Guide to the Archeology of Tomorrow* [1981], Abbeville Press (New York), 1982.
3. Gilles Deleuze and Félix Guattari, *A Thousand Plateaus: Capitalism and Schizophrenia* [1980], tr. Brian Massumi, University of Minnesota Press (Minneapolis), 1987, pp. 88–91.
4. Lewis Mumford, *Technics and Civilization*, Harcourt, Brace & Company (New York), 1934, pp. 109–32.

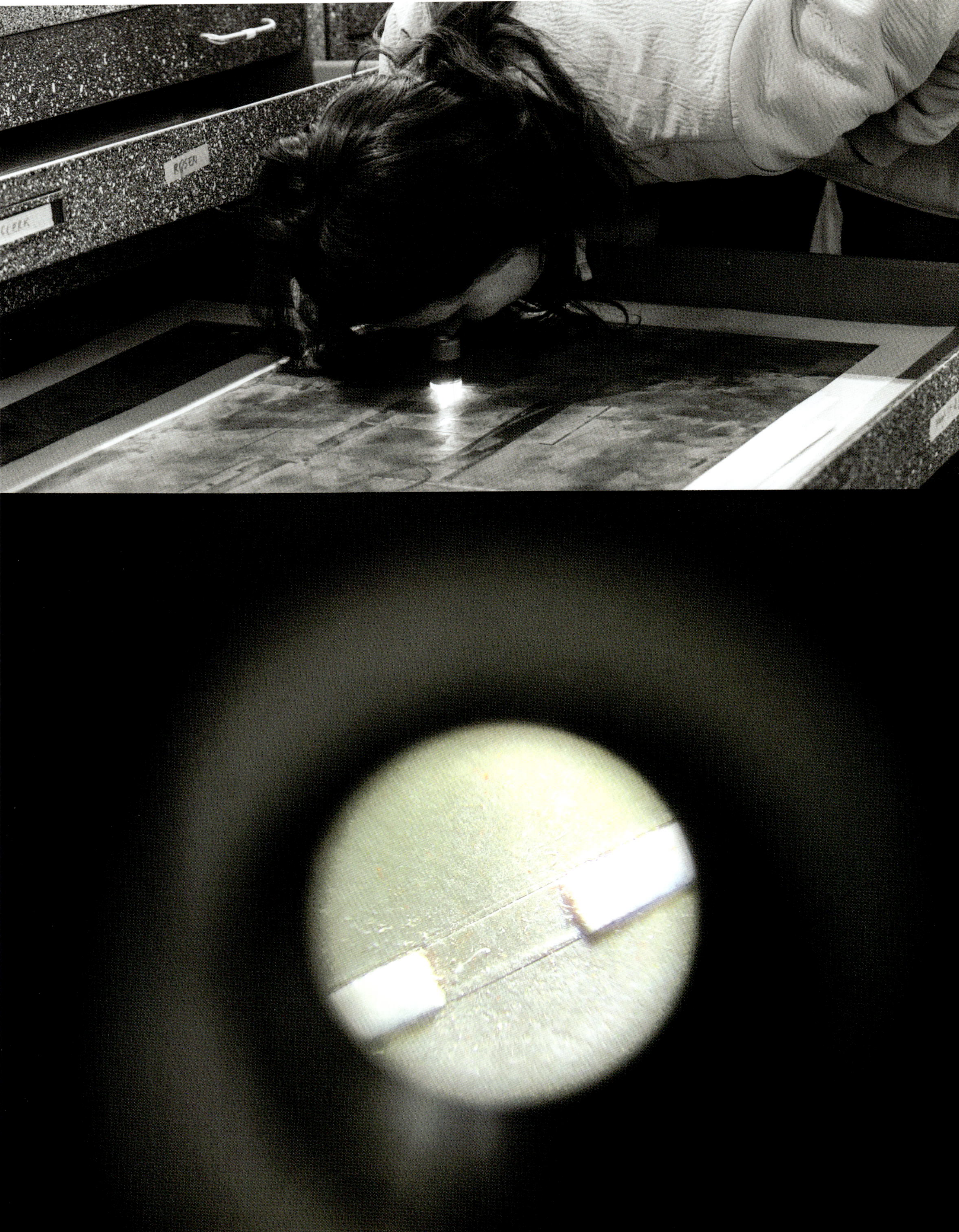

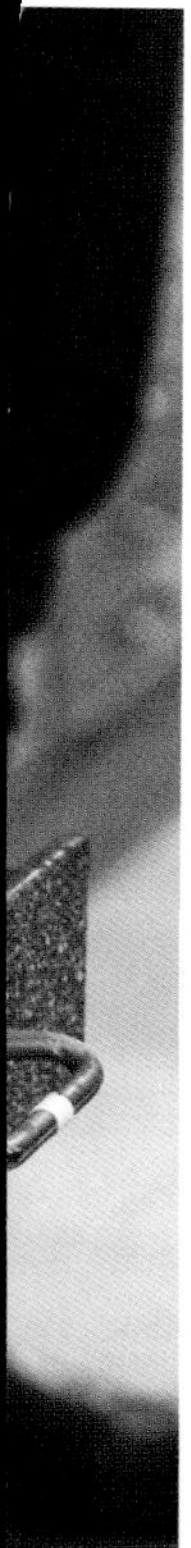

Aleksandra Wagner

Saving What Is Vibrant, Tracing What Remains

Inspired by the aura of Morphosis prints held at A83 and desiring to extend its possibilities, Belgium-based architect and educator Riet Eeckhout employs drawing as a mode of seeing, tracing, remembering, and forgetting. Conversing with Eeckhout's project, **Aleksandra Wagner** attempts to get beneath the surface of this mournful research marked on the pale and smooth Mylar, a substance mute yet mutating.

Thom Mayne / Morphosis,
The Kate Mantilini,
The Lifeguard Station,
1988

Close up—Riet Eeckhout enters the drawing by examining its depth. A magnified dashed line in the modeling paste applied to the print casts a shadow on the layer beneath. Its spatiality opens up to the viewer; the traces of technique become visible.

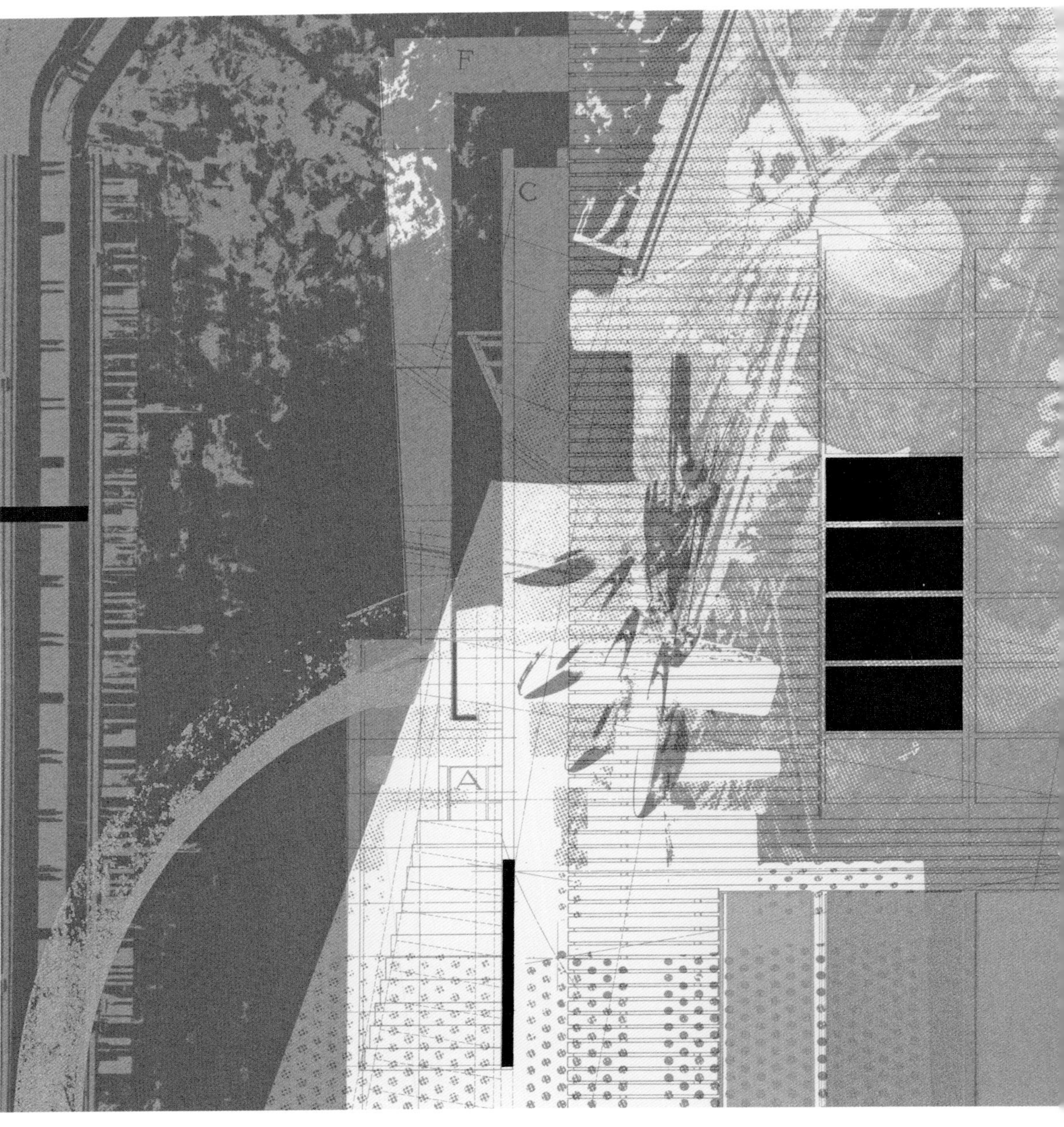

Thom Mayne / Morphosis,
5th of June,
1989

The original state of the
print with which Eeckhout
chose to work. Comprising
multiple screenprinted layers,
it uses different kinds of
representational techniques
to produce a disjunctive
composite image.

In the winter of 2023, when a group of architects was invited to study the expansive archive of New York gallery and printmaking studio A83 to choose the work they found resonant and do something with it, the mode of doing was left open. Folded into this was another invitation—for a projection of personal sensibility and medium into a new one, that of print.

Riet Eeckhout, an Associate Professor at the KU Leuven, Belgium, and a researcher who draws, exhibits, and writes from within the discipline of architecture, focused on two images by Thom Mayne / Morphosis: *The Kate Mantilini, The Lifeguard Station* (1988) and *5th of June* (1989).

Thickness

The choice of *The Kate Mantilini, The Lifeguard Station* was partially guided by thickness. For those who do not think of drawings as thick, the word "thickness" might sound odd. Yet, with a tiny tool and a less-than-tiny dose of inquisitiveness, it is possible to shine light into the layered mysteries of "below." Seen through the magnifying lens, a dashed line casts a shadow; a space, otherwise hidden from the naked eye, that is 3.5 millimeters deep. The promise of entering a drawing—its power augmented by the vulnerability of a slightly injured edge—is being set up.

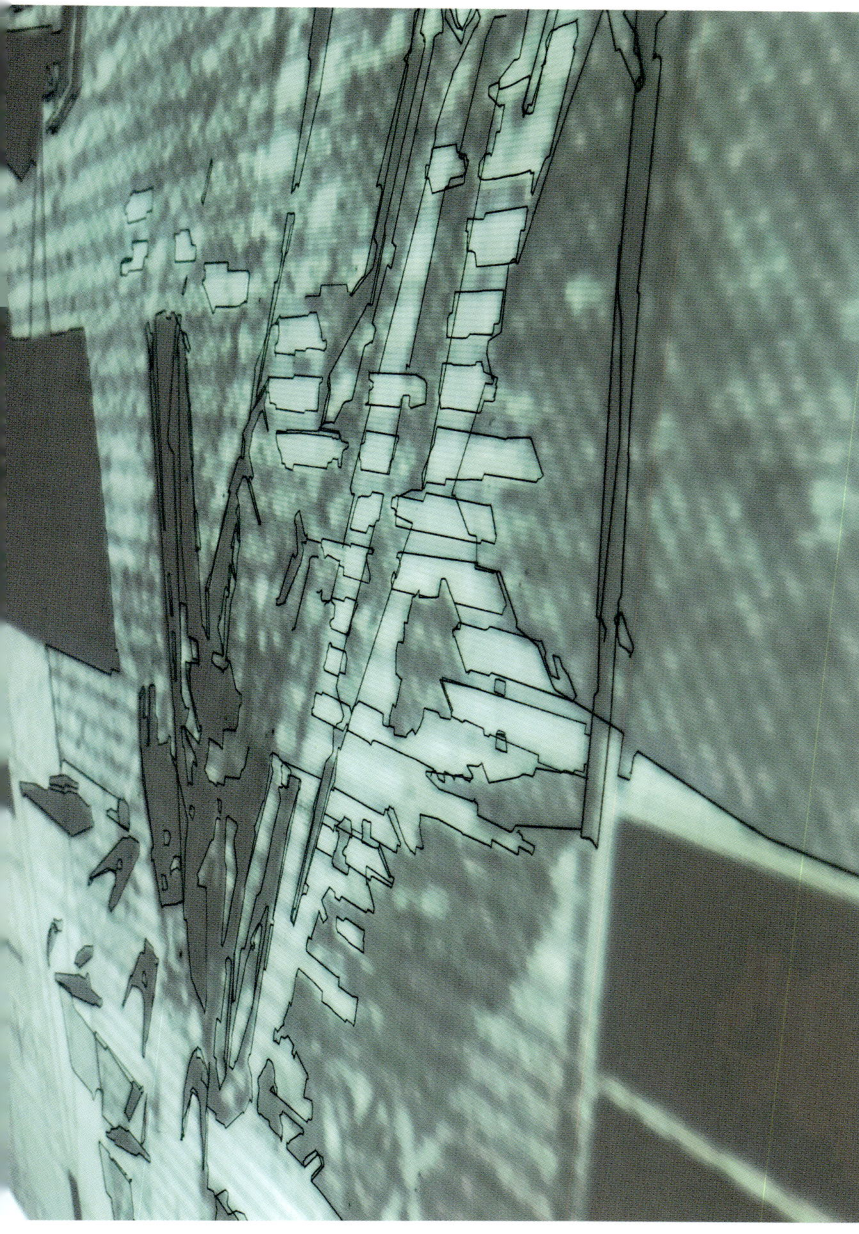

Getting closer to the particulars of the fragmented body. An oblique monochrome photograph of the drawing process teases out the spatial disposition of Thom Mayne / Morphosis's *5th of June* print. Pencil lines demarcate surface and tonal differences.

Resisting Objecthood

This is not the first time for Eeckhout to be drawn to the lines of an Other. The doings of others interest her; she summons them into her service and caringly extracts the "spatial content out of existing situations."[1] Between 2017 and 2022 she worked on a material dialogue with a sketch deposited in the collection of Alvin Boyarsky.[2] That, too, was an invitation requiring a response. Conversing with Frank Gehry—drawing him out of the archival silence—Eeckhout chose a moment, perhaps of the author's "explanation" of something to someone: nothing to do with the building, at least not representationally. She took up a left-behind extension of an architect's mind, a repository of spatial thinking independent of any-body's claims of architecture as property and affirmed again that entering a drawing is possible. She found her way by trusting the intuitiveness of engagement; by placing herself in the center; by sometimes not listening to the drawing at all.

Here Eeckhout intuits, finds, and values the depths of what for some others appears as a flat surface. She takes thickness to be the site for speculative archaeology that allows for the definition of architecture as *an immersive activity*. Not surprisingly, the process of drawing becomes *a productive resistance*, in which there is no blank slate, but also no filial piety. Things have always been with us (and may have decayed), but such remnants are not where the architecture resides. Better to think of architecture as a space in between: a relational environment. The in-between where all shifts occur is far more telling than any fixed form. The dynamism of in between-ness saves what is vibrant—a drawing, as well as architecture—from becoming an object.

The experiential nature of the encounter, its spatial disposition, is
central to her quest: the simultaneity of exploring form and change, of
receiving a trace of the passing and giving back to it

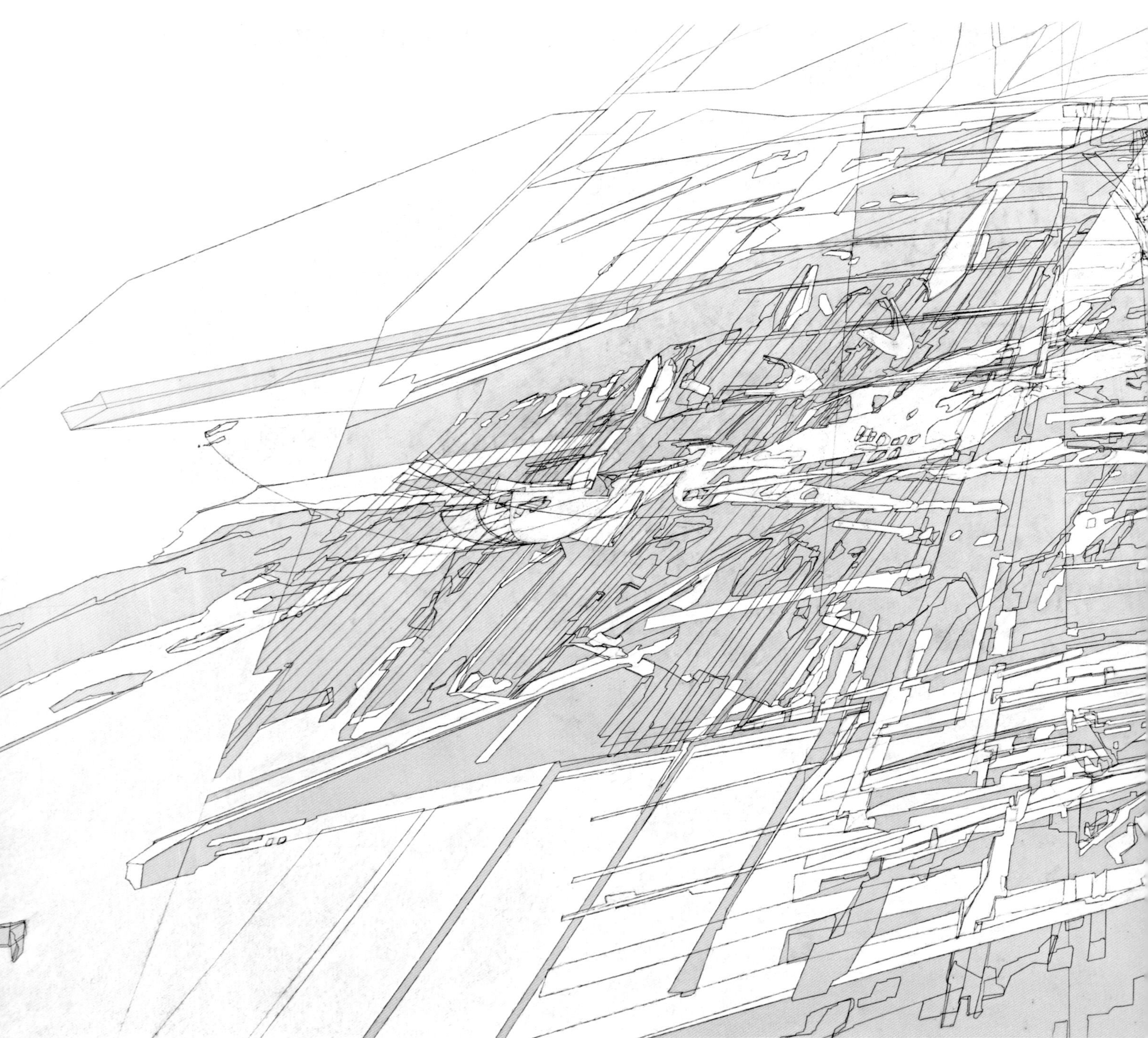

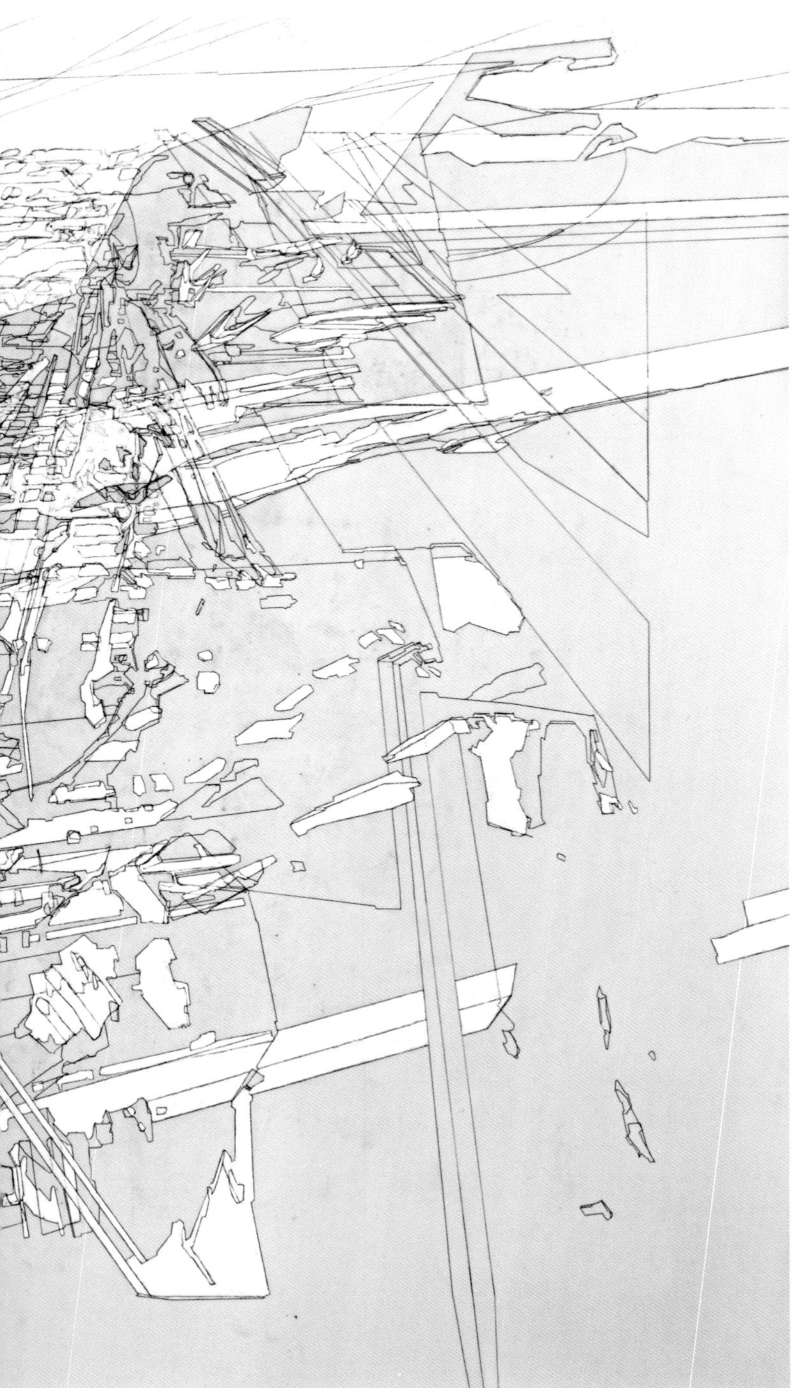

If *The Kate Mantilini, The Lifeguard Station* provoked thoughts about thickness, *5th of June* poses questions at a different scale. Suspended between the memory of Mayne's hand and Eeckhout's move toward and away from it, the observer might be tempted to inquire about her object devotion, even about her voluminous capacity to mourn. Eeckhout would likely respond by saying that *it*, the starting point, *merely looks like an object*—yet is always containing multiplicities, sedimented processes, interiorities made of gaps and cracks. For Eeckhout, a ground that invites with a promise of stability ultimately speaks to the inevitability of transience.

If *it* merely looks like an object while not necessarily being an object, what is Eeckhout after? Perhaps she is after learning how to resist the very idea of objecthood while dealing with the entanglements of authorship and resisting those, too. Or, closer to her own words, she may be after the critical surrender to the drawing— the one already existent and the one to come. What she is *not* after is the inquiry into what a drawing is "about"; *not* after what some term its "meaning." The experiential nature of the encounter, its spatial disposition, is central to her quest: the simultaneity of exploring form and change, of receiving a trace of the passing and giving back to it.

She is after a haunting doubleness.

Mute, Pale, and Smooth

Describing Mylar as "mute, pale and smooth,"[3] Eeckhout lets us closer to her intimate armamentarium. With it, this is how a non-linear progress of the *5th of June* might unfold: Look slowly. Add a triangle, a pencil, and a white marker. Proceed by using a camera lens and think of the oblique views and orthogonality. Now project the photograph onto the Mylar, already on a drawing board of no miniscule size, and recall that projection is a big word in Eeckhout's glossary of means. (She may be counting in millimeters, but her manner is a blow-up. What starts as smaller is bound to expand.) Better

yet: make a film or use a readymade so you can think with time. Let a celluloid or something less flammable (a ray of light) merge with the polyester. Having made the starting material elusive and yet so close to hand, you may be freed from the habit. Trace what you grasp as visible. With some luck, you may also be freed from the contexts and their values.

Like Eeckhout, you may choose to lay Mayne's verticality down. And, just like she does, you may impose on yourself a terrifying rule: to erase nothing.

It takes a fool to ask where, in this process, which Eeckhout refuses to

call "transformation," is the power of the previous maker. Still, was Mayne hovering over her shoulders? What about the title, *5th of June*, and its year of creation, 1989? Eeckhout shifts to numbers only. *8965* is the title now. What, or who, is the Subject then? And, if there is one, what anxieties might they induce or receive?

Riet Eeckhout,
8965 (screenprint),
both sides,
2025

right: A haunting doubleness—the solemnness of the print departs from the drawing's willful innocence. The silkscreen print was produced by printing three separations on either side of a Mylar sheet.

Riet Eeckhout,
8965, oblique detail
photograph,
2025

above left: Eeckhout used a
sequence of photographs, of
which this is one example,
to construct two kinds of
projection, which appeared
on the front and back of the
screenprint. The screenprint
was produced on transparent
Mylar so the relation between
the two projections could be
read on either side.

Riet Eeckhout,
Study for 8965
(screenprint),
2025

above right: A process drawing
made in order to study the
treatment for one of the sides
of the screenprint. Eeckhout
is layering modeling paste on
the front and the back of the
Mylar sheet. Thom Mayne /
Morphosis had used modeling
paste on their *The Kate
Mantilini, The Lifeguard Station*
print. This technique provoked
Eeckhout's own interest in
layering and the question of
the depth of the drawing.

The printer's frames with
an Eeckhout trace,
February 2025

Eeckhout's image caught on the
photo-exposed screens from
which the layers are printed.
What we see are the front and
back of a single separation that
defines one color. A shadow of
an object: dust to dust.

Emptying the Subject

The invitation conveyed by A83 can
be understood in at least two ways.
One would be to think of an extension
of what already exists, if through an
undercurrent of memorialization;
despite the challenges and resistances,
the genealogical line may appear as
seamless. Another would be to think
through a lens of the future-directed
consideration, of *what the print*—as
opposed to Louis Kahn's brick,[4] or even
a drawing—*wants to be*. In this sense,
the invitation interrupts; this time,
due to the challenges and resistances,
the line may become jagged. Here
Eeckhout converses with Thom Mayne
on a different plane. Defining the aims
of Morphosis in 1993 (reflecting on
their work of the previous decade),
he wrote that we must strive to see
"anew: unexpected, everchanging
patterns altered by time appear in the
places we thought we understood."[5]

It might be useful to think of *8965*
in terms of its relationship to a legacy.
Indeed, what is Eeckhout's continual
engagement with the work of others
asking us to reflect on? If such an
engagement were linked solely to
the "cases" of Gehry and Mayne,
we could choose to call it a respect
for the (male) ancestors. But her
engagement is not that narrow. She
finds the work of others to be a zone
of the unknown, a spring generating
energy and therefore the foundation
of her own epistemology and creative
labor. Instead of relying on the
common understanding of processes
of internalization, which sometimes
substitutes imitation with influence,
Eeckhout makes it explicit that she is
a thinking and feeling vessel for an
Otherness of the past.

When asked how it feels to be working off the work of others, and how it felt to take the next step through which a drawing will become a print, Eeckhout's response was that—somewhat irrespective of the material to be put to use—she wants to know, already knows, must know more, about the person behind it. It is a response of a "student," for whom not every "teacher" is equally good. The composite narrative matters and moves her as the point of departure. We could quickly conclude that the Author matters, that it is the Author that she needs to hold on to.

But to be quick is often to be wrong. There is a moment when the projector is turned off and when the projections—visual, aural, textual—join each other's company. We sit then with what we know, and meet the unknowability of the Other on such terms. At that turning point, legacy fades into a background. A trace on what is *mute, pale, and smooth* is all there is, and can now be turned into the Subject; we listen no longer to anything else but to ourselves. In the murmur of Roland Barthes, "it is language that speaks, not the author."[6]

To That Moment
It might also be useful to think of *8965* in terms of its relationship to the printing atelier. Eeckhout sees it as the site where the agency of a drawer is given up, with and despite all efforts at collaboration. For the print to happen, some drawn lines are chosen over others. The authority of that selective act, layered both literally and metaphorically, is not captured as much in the printer's choice of color or in a slight shift in scale, as in the self-consciousness of the small drawing made to serve as a guide for an archaeology of the print—a new "thickness"—to be established. With further extraction of the field from within the field, the large-scale drawing loses its innocence through the detail. A printer's proof becomes the proof that our unconscious cannot be offered freely.

Speaking about her work, Eeckhout has commented on the question asked by a viewer: "When is the drawing finished?"[7] She responded by suggesting that the question of when something stops, even if it does not end, might be closer to her experience than any hint about finitude. The arc connecting Thom Mayne / Morphosis, Riet Eeckhout, and A83, may be leading to the same conclusion. The serigraphed Mayne / Morphosis drawing stopped only to be reprojected into a drawing on Mylar that stopped only to be reprojected into a print and laid in the box: an object now obligated to disclaim its objectivity.

For, in the poignant words of John Berger, "objectivity is what is left when something is finished."[8] ⚗

Notes
1. Mark Dorrian, Riet Eeckhout, and Arnaud Hendrickx (eds.), *Drawing Architecture: Conversations on Contemporary Practice*, Lund Humphries (London), 2022, p. 105.
2. Eeckhout's series "Drawing Out Gehry I–VIII" (2017–22) was published in Michael McGarry, "Shallow to Deep: Drawing as Close Encounter," in Neil Spiller (ed.), ⚗ *Radical Architectural Drawing*, July/August (no.4), 2022, pp. 38–45.
3. Dorrian, Eeckhout, and Hendrickx, *Drawing Architecture*, p. 98.
4. Louis I. Kahn, "I Love Beginnings," speech given at the International Design Conference, Aspen, Colorado, 1972, in Alessandra Latour (ed.), *Louis I. Kahn: Writings, Lectures, Interviews*, Rizzoli (New York), 1991, p. 288.
5. Thom Mayne, "Connected Isolation," in Morphosis, *Connected Isolation*, ⚗ Monograph No. 23, Academy Editions (London), 1993, p. 10.
6. Roland Barthes, "The Death of the Author" [1967], in *Image, Music, Text*, tr. Stephen Heath, Fontana (London), 1977, p. 143.
7. Dorrian, Eeckhout, and Hendrickx, *Drawing Architecture*, p. 102.
8. John Berger, "Drawn to that Moment," in *The Sense of Sight*, Pantheon Books (New York), 1985, p. 147.

Bea Martin

Blue in the Wild

Sir Peter Cook's Endless Play of Hide and Seek

Sir Peter Cook,
Glimpses of the City,
2023

opposite: Cook here plays with the elusiveness of the urban fragment, where controlled vegetation moves and invites play. The city becomes a backdrop, glimpsed through slits and apertures, with architecture framed as something to be pursued, not simply seen.

Sir Peter Cook,
Growth City, "Sixth Somewhat Annual Meeting"
exhibition, A83 gallery,
New York,
2025

left: *Growth City* begins with a clear, orthogonal grid, gradually unraveling into branching, tree-like forms. Whether these elements are truly growing, or simply mimicking growth, is left unresolved, an ambiguity that is part of the drawing's power, where architecture and nature metabolize into one another.

Looking back over the work of someone like Peter Cook, who has been speculating about architecture and cities for more than 65 years, offers new inspiration from previous and long-lasting preoccupations. His work has flirted with ideas of metamorphosis, of playful, fluctuating translucence, and of abundant Arcadian landscapes providing the biological impetus for change. London-based architect and educator **Bea Martin** waxes lyrically and appreciatively on Cook's visionary vitality and continual architectural experimentation.

Blue is a quiet anomaly in nature. It does not come easily, nor does it sit obediently within the spectrum of the ordinary. It is neither the ochres of the earth nor the verdant hues borne of chlorophyll's abundance. Blue is a color that must be conjured rather than simply found. And yet, every so often, blue appears in the wild—a streak of electric iridescence on a morpho butterfly's wing, the impossible shimmer of a kingfisher in flight, the startling presence of a cobalt bloom in a field of green. These are not accidents. These are acts of visual rebellion, blue as defiance, blue as spectacle, blue as an assertion that some things are not meant to blend in.

Sir Peter Cook is such a presence—a rare flash of blue in a discipline so often resigned to the muted tones of pragmatism. His architectural drawings do not submit to conventional representation; they flicker, vibrate, and hover in and out of certainty. Lines are twitchy. Color refuses to behave, and space never quite holds still. His drawings are provocations, invitations, agitations—gardens of pure potential where architecture teases, transforms, and resists finality.

To understand Cook's drawings is to inhabit his mind, decode his very own vocabulary, one built of fragments—pieces that shift, reappear, and collide to form architectures of endless possibility. But not all fragments behave the same way. Some are undefined, slipping between presence and absence, refusing to fully appear. Others perform, stepping forward boldly, demanding to be seen. Some are restless, caught mid-transformation, neither arriving nor departing. And others represent fragments of fragments, broken apart and reassembled, as a collage of architectural memory.

Like blue in the wild, Cook's drawings are mysterious, playing between revelation and concealment, never seeking resolution but reveling in the endless pleasure of becoming—an ever-shifting assembly of fragments that construct worlds in flux, where nothing is fixed, and everything is alive with possibility.

Now You See Me, Now You Don't

Peter Cook's worlds are built on the joy of indecision—where every edge is an invitation rather than a boundary. His drawings trace, shuffle, and dissolve into an organic latticework of their own making. In *Glimpses of the City* (2023) and *Growth City* (2024), the urban fragment becomes an active agent—something that teases, transforms, and always keeps moving. These are not depictions of fixed architecture, but cities in performance, oscillating between concealment and revelation.

In *Glimpses of the City*, the fragment is elusive—a trickster caught between the seen and unseen. "It's a game of screens," Cook reflects. "Controlled vegetation—growing—that aren't wild but aren't rigidly artificial either. They move. They invite play." Architecture is glanced at through composed slits and apertures, pursued rather than presented. What lies behind, he suggests, is "a predictable city"—but it is the act of hiding and revealing that generates a more compelling urban condition. The veils of foliage do not obscure; they activate.

If *Glimpses of the City* is about searching, *Growth City* is about surrender. Here, the drawing evolves from a grid—a megastructure, something orthogonal—into branching, vegetal formations. "It begins to break down," Cook explains, "to evolve into tree-like structures." The result is a speculative system of urban growth, where scaffold becomes tendril, and the built dissolves into organic logic. His process is instinctive, assembled through controlled disjunction. "There's a definite scale in my head," he notes, pointing to a cargo ship tucked into the scene—a familiar anchor within the drawing's entangled ecology. The hexagonal framing acts as a spatial trap, tilting toward the viewer, subtly implying that we are not just looking in—we are already inside.

Sir Peter Cook,
The Garden is the City,
2025

In *The Garden is the City*, Cook envisions
architecture as a precise, curated vessel.
Vegetation pours through every crevice, merging
with monumental forms and market stalls alike.
The orange sky becomes a stage, where towers
and façades perform in a carefully orchestrated
blend of structure and cultivated nature.

BUBBLE SUBURB
PETER COOK 2025

His refusal to draw digitally is not a limitation, but a mode of resistance. Unbound by sequential rules, the hand becomes a site of improvisation. At "The Sixth Somewhat Annual Meeting" exhibition at the A83 gallery, New York, *Growth City* was reimagined through print—not as a fixed artifact, but as an open-ended architectural proposition. The drawing was translated through Risograph printing, where misregistration, vivid overlays, and material idiosyncrasies echoed the drawing's own logic of shift and slip. The print became an experimental site, transforming reproduction into speculation.

For Cook, the exhibition context—shared with peers he admires—recalled the charged dynamic of a competitive studio. "It's a bit like being in school again," he admits. "You feel the urge to parry—to raise your game." But more than competition, it was a call to risk—to step beyond the comforts of the academic and into public view. "The greatest danger for the adult architect is to become an imitator of oneself," he notes. *Growth City*, like the exhibition itself, is a refusal of that ambush—a drawing in perpetual formation, always on the cusp of becoming something else.

Somewhere Between Streetlight and Sunlight

Cook's cities are not fixed locations; they are performances—compositions of fragments that thrive on disruption and revel in transformation. *The Garden is the City* (2025) and *Bubble Suburb* (2025) unfold as two distinct urban acts: one a structured spectacle eager to be seen, the other a soft, murmuring drift dissolving into its own terrain.

In *The Garden is the City*, the fragment becomes a controlled vessel where architecture asserts itself with clarity. "It's about the garden as the city," Cook muses. There is no boundary between the two—vegetation spills into every crevice, cascading from monumental forms into the urban fabric. The city is an orchestrated interplay of structure and cultivated nature, where even the market stall in the foreground is laced with greenery. Above, the orange sky is not mere atmosphere but theatrical—a glowing stage upon which crystalline towers, tensile canopies, and biomorphic façades perform. Here, curation is deliberate, elements placed with precision rather than left to dissolve.

Where its counterpart sharpens, *Bubble Suburb* dissolves—resisting definition. "I started off with a rule," Cook explains, "where the walls of the domes could peel off, snake around, and wrap into the next dome along." Instead of discrete structures, these forms move like a ribboning landscape, clinging, unfolding, expanding. Cook delights in the name—*Bubble Suburb*—which dictated the presence of a rigid, rectilinear skyline against which the swelling, gelatinous terrain could be distinguished. "I deliberately made the city predictable," he notes, its grid a counterpoint to the bubbling sprawl. Towers emerge reluctantly: "I needed them—a punctuation, a rhythm to stop the bubbles from becoming indigestible, like a sentence with no breaks."

These drawings embody Cook's fascination with the city—sometimes structured, sometimes seeping, but always unfixed. One learns how to be seen; the other learns how to disappear. Between them, no finality—only the joy of perpetual transformation.

Sir Peter Cook,
Bubble Suburb,
2025

Bubble Suburb resists definition, opting for fluidity over formality. It begins with a simple rule: domes that peel, snake, and wrap into one another—forming a continuous, swelling terrain. This softness is set against a rigid skyline, framing the suburban sprawl with deliberate contrast.

Landscapes That Won't Sit Still

Cook's landscapes are never finished—they are acts of continuous assembly, terrains caught mid-shift, refusing to be resolved into a single state. *Fissure* (2024) and *Inclusive Landscape* (2023) capture two distinct yet equally restless conditions: one is a weave, a layering of terrains that absorb, expand, and evolve; the other is a rupture, a jagged split that cuts deep into the land, swallowing architecture into a theater of tension. Although anchored, neither landscape is moored.

In *Fissure*, the landscape is already dramatic, a deep chasm where architecture clings to the cliffs, uncertain of its own permanence. "I take what is already an event—the fissure itself— and let the architecture react to it," Cook explains. The result is a tectonic drama, where fairytale-like structures merge into the

verticality of the valley, some half-exposed, others veiled behind a skin of greenery and glass. "Are you looking at a mountain, or a giant concealed apartment block?," he says, as he wittily points out a patch of vegetation that doubles as a glazed façade, blurring the line between building and terrain. Color here is sharp, separating elements, carving out the void, making absence feel as present as form.

By contrast, *Inclusive Landscape* does not break—it thickens. It is not a theater of rupture but a landscape of layering, where architecture does not impose itself but seeps into the terrain. "I've done imagined landscapes for years," Cook reflects, tracing his fascination back to his "Mounds and Lumps" in the 1970s— drawings of artificial hills where fragments of architecture peeked through. "The game is about embedding architecture

into the land—sometimes it disappears, sometimes it accents the terrain, sometimes it barely reveals itself at all." In *Inclusive Landscape*, there is no single event, no one feature that demands attention. The land itself is fluid, an ongoing negotiation between movement, sediment, and built form. The eye does not fall into an abyss but instead wanders, following fast-moving rivers, hilltops, and shifting geological seams.

Both drawings explore the fate of architecture in the landscape. In *Fissure*, the city clings on, negotiating survival. In *Inclusive Landscape*, the city dissolves, learning to merge with time itself. Whether embedded, veiled, or left barely perceptible, Cook's fragments resist resolution—always shifting, always playing hide-and-seek with the land that holds them.

Sir Peter Cook,
Fissure,
2024

opposite: Cook here begins with the drama of the landscape itself—an event—and lets tne architecture respond. Structures cling to the cliffs, half-veiled by greenery and glass, blurring the line between mountain and building. Bold color carves out the void, making absence as vivid as form.

Sir Peter Cook,
Inclusive Landscape,
2023

above: Rupture is avoided here in favor of accumulation. Architecture is embedded into the land. The drawing thickens rather than breaks, blending form with terrain. There is no single focal point—just a fluid negotiation of rivers, seams, and soft hilltops that invite the eye to wander.

Sir Peter Cook,
City Mix,
2024

City Mix reads like a ruin in motion—a city shedding its framework as tectonic forms drift and dissolve. Buildings lose their sharpness, grid lines bend, and vegetation takes over, softening the edges. Cook describes it as an experiment, a set of fragments that resist resolution.

Through the Echo of Their Own Making

Cook's buildings do not stand still—they melt, erupt, scatter, and accumulate. *City Mix* (2024) and *Downtown* (2024) are restless compositions where fragments misbehave, and color surges in unexpected directions. One is in slow-motion collapse, its grid dissolving, its logic unraveling. The other is a vertical fever dream, stacking higher, expanding outward in a riot of excess. Neither follows inevitability; both exist in the sheer delight of becoming.

In *City Mix*, the fragment is a ruin in motion. "This was an experiment," Cook admits. "A mix of tectonic forms layered into an organic drift." Buildings soften, grid lines waver, and vegetation swallows hard edges. The city sheds its framework, its rules dissolving into architectural hesitation. "I wasn't even sure if I liked it," he muses, "but I followed through with it." Pink auditoria nestle between boxy housing blocks, while a municipal dome, oddly nostalgic, lingers like a misplaced relic. Waterfalls cascade onto entrances, blurring the boundary between erosion and design. "They're really just vignettes," Cook reflects. "They don't add up to a coherent proposition— that is me, playing with vocabulary."

Refusing decay, *Downtown* condenses with ambition. This city does not dissolve but metastasizes—a vertical improvisation of scaffolds, crystalline spires, and tensile membranes. "This one is more to my taste," Cook notes, favoring slivers, fissures, and insertions. Unlike *City Mix*, which drifts between styles, *Downtown* builds upon itself with relentless momentum. "Many surfaces aren't even impervious," Cook observes. "Some might be translucent, some flimsy, implying a city inside a vast installation, under an invisible dome." It marks his return to collage after 30 years; "I struggled to find bright enough material," he recounts, lamenting the muted palettes of contemporary print culture.

Between erosion and accumulation, these cities are not places but forces—always shifting, assembling, and on the verge of something else.

Blue Never Fades

For Cook, fragments are not merely components of a drawing; they are the very syntax through which architecture materializes—not as a static entity, but as an unfolding dialogue. To draw is to assemble, to shape a world that exists in flux, where forms emerge, dissolve, and reconfigure in an endless negotiation between becoming and unbecoming. Sir Peter Cook's drawings remind us that architecture is not a fixed object but a field of play—an ever-shifting terrain where nothing holds still, everything is in motion, and composition is an act of perpetual reinvention. In this world, blue—always the quiet anomaly—never recedes, never conforms. It lingers, flickers, asserts itself, just as Cook's visions do, vivid, elusive, and impossible to pin down. ◌

All quotes in this article are from a conversation between the Bea Martin and Peter Cook in March 2025

Sir Peter Cook,
Downtown,
2024

In *Downtown*, Cook returned to collage after 30 years, with a vertical improvisation of scaffolds, spires, and tensile membranes, built with momentum rather than drift. Surfaces remain uncertain, implying a city within a vast, invisible installation.

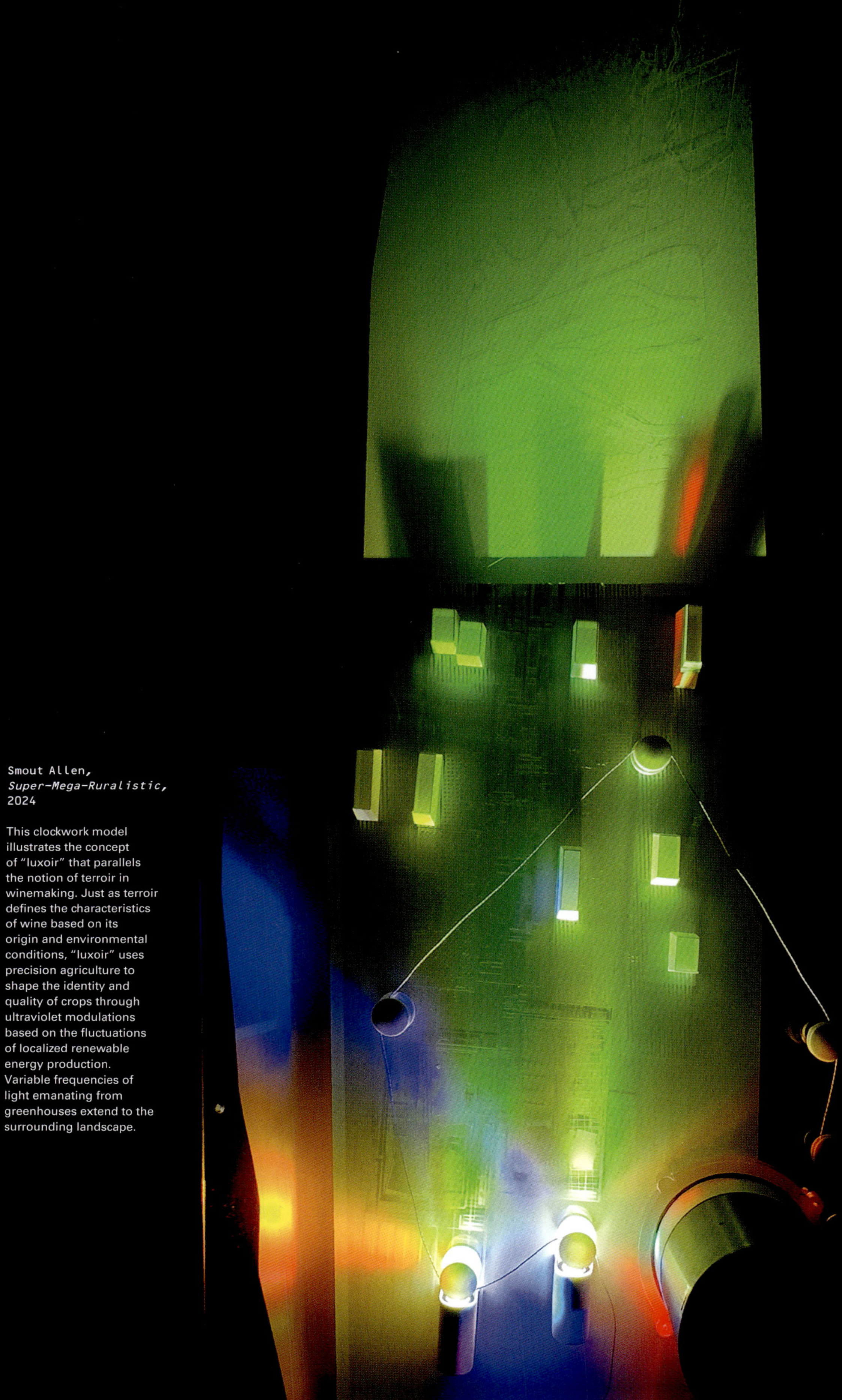

This clockwork model illustrates the concept of "luxoir" that parallels the notion of terroir in winemaking. Just as terroir defines the characteristics of wine based on its origin and environmental conditions, "luxoir" uses precision agriculture to shape the identity and quality of crops through ultraviolet modulations based on the fluctuations of localized renewable energy production. Variable frequencies of light emanating from greenhouses extend to the surrounding landscape.

Stan Allen

Thin Strings of Hue

SMOUT ALLEN'S SUPER-MEGA-RURALISTIC LANDSCAPES

Producing an architectural drawing by hand is a time-consuming activity—it is procedural, involving conventions of notation. It can also be a free-flowing nexus of color and line, created in a kind of graphic dance. The drawings and prints of Bartlett Professors Mark Smout and Laura Allen (Smout Allen) have such a choreography of joy, originality, and discovery. Princeton Emeritus Professor **Stan Allen** examines their modus operandi, and elucidates their creative landscape aspirations for us.

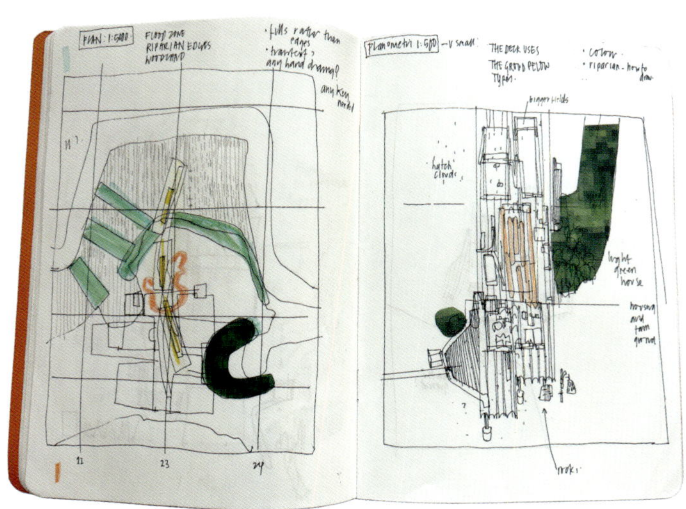

Sketches for a series of scaled plan drawings that reveal the evolving territorial conditions under flood and drought, and the spatial choreography of field systems and domestic enclosures.

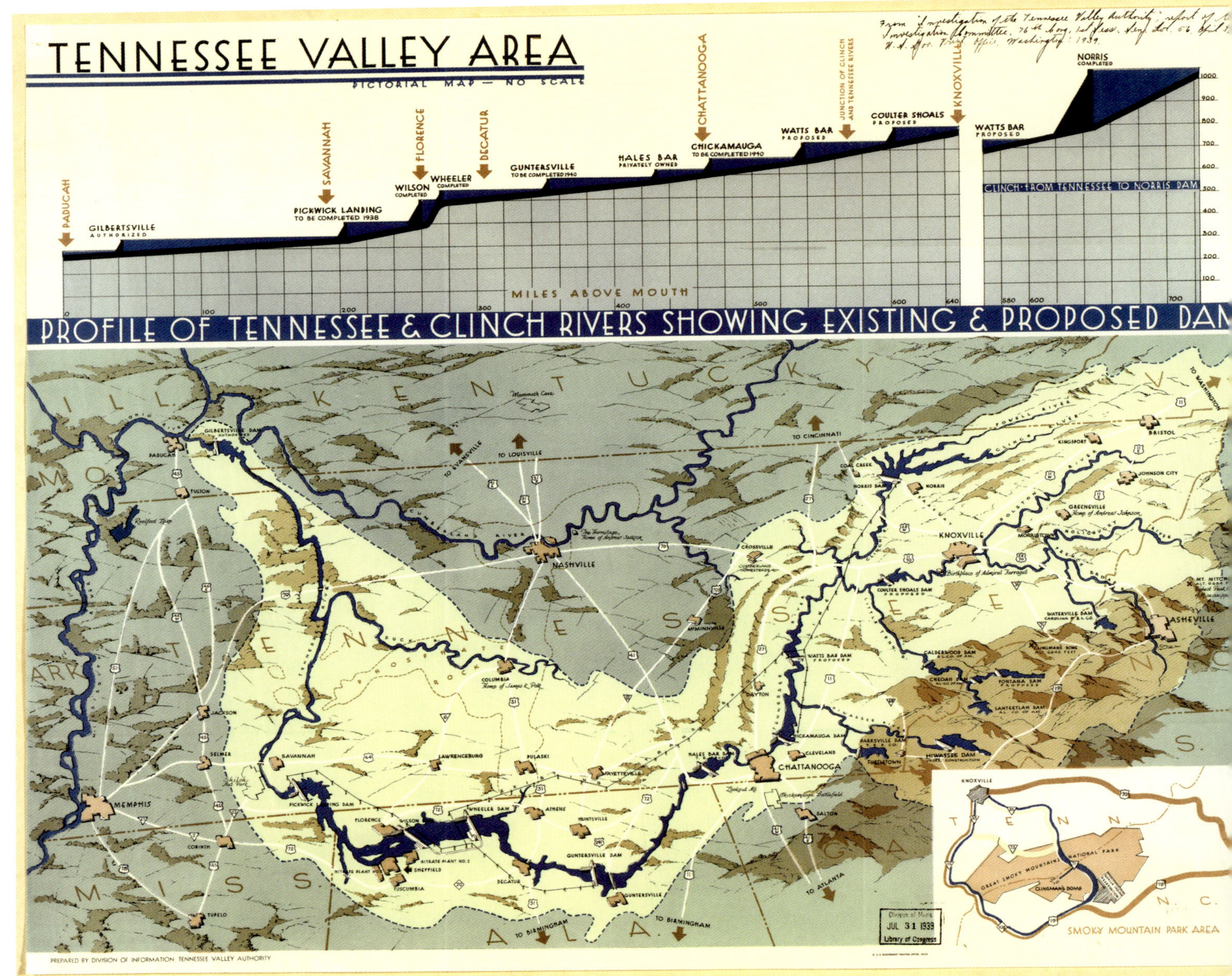

Tennessee Valley Authority,
Pictorial map of Tennessee and Clinch
Rivers showing existing and proposed dams,
1939

The Tennessee Valley Authority's large-scale regional
planning scheme focused on flood control, electricity
generation, agricultural improvement, and economic
development. It reshaped the Tennessee River system,
constructing a series of dams and hydroelectric plants
and controlling 11,000 miles of shoreline. (From
"Investigation of the Tennessee Valley Authority,"
report of the Investigation Committee, 76th Congress,
1st Session, April 3, 1939, US Government Printing
Office (Washington, D.C.), 1939.)

Furthermore, every color is a completed presence in the world, a recognizable being apart from any object, while a few odd lines (since a line is only an artificial edge) are: nothing—thin strings of hue.
— William Gass, *On Being Blue*, 1976[1]

Buildings are not black lines on white paper.
— Zoe Zenghelis, "Roosevelt Island," 2019[2]

Line or color? *Disegno* or *colore*? The debate was thoroughly aired. Ingres and Delacroix in the 19th century, Poussin and Rubens in the 17th, and before that, Renaissance Florentines and Venetians. In the *Critique of Aesthetic Judgment* (1790), the German philosopher Immanuel Kant gave his verdict: "In painting, sculpture, and in fact in all the formative arts, in architecture and horticulture, in so far as they are fine arts, the *design* is what is essential."[3] Design—by which he means the clear delineation of form and the ordered arrangement of two- and three-dimensional space— is rational, and imparts consistency to the painting, the building, the garden. But for Venetian painters such as Titian and Tintoretto, line and color could never be separated. There are no lines in nature, and no lines in sumptuously rendered drapery or a diaphanous cloud against a luminous blue sky. Color imparts sensuality and emotion to a painting, drawing the viewer in. To its critics, color is seductive, but insufficient on its own—cosmetic, applied after the fact. It must be subordinated to the discipline of line and contour. Color is irrational, they argue, and the atmospherics of color cloud the mind. Line is masculine; color is feminine; fickle and promiscuous. Competing concepts

of nature are at work here—one of underlying geometric structure, the other of the bright surface of things.

It was one of those debates in which each side states their case with unassailable logic, holds tenaciously to their position, and nobody ever changes their mind. "A thing well-drawn is always a thing well-painted," declared Ingres,[4] to which Delacroix answered, "the enemy of all painting is grey."[5]

Unsurprisingly, for the Italian Renaissance architect and theorist Leon Battista Alberti, *disegno* is primary. Color hardly enters the picture. "Building is a form of body," he writes, "which like any other consists of lineaments and matter."[6] Lineaments are a product of thought, aligned with the mind and the power of reason; matter derives from nature: raw, unformed, disordered. And in the 20th century, Le Corbusier (despite employing color freely in his own buildings) recommended a coat of whitewash to banish the unclean and the disorderly: "Every citizen is required to replace his hangings, his damasks, his wallpapers, his stencils, with a plain coat of white *ripolin*."[7] No more decoration, no more dark corners, everything shown just as it is. Le Corbusier may have spent his mornings painting, but in his written propositions he relentlessly subordinated the accidental and the circumstantial to a generalized and abstract idea of order.

This digressive starting point springs from my intuition that the work of Smout Allen is animated by a productive interplay between line and color. Not the simultaneous execution of *colore* and *disegno* argued for by Titian, but a kind of dance: two equal partners smoothly trading off, making subtle adjustments, and responding to every movement made by the other. In this regard it is significant that Smout Allen, bypassing what has become standard practice today, never

construct axonometrics as computer models captured as views but always directly in the drawing, leading to distortions and inconsistencies, to layerings and complexities, which are for them the happy accidents that both enable invention and impart a vibrancy to the drawings. These drawings are alive—not only with the trace of the author's hand (because their mode of working maintains a certain remove), but with all the complexity, unpredictability, and inconsistency of the real, of a thing made by living human beings.

Architecture's monochrome palette may have begun to open up in the 1960s (the Kodachrome universe of Superstudio's photocollages, the Pop Art colors of Archigram), but it is important to remember that until architects began to use graphic software, it was not so easy to get color into an architectural drawing. Applying color to a drawing required architects to step outside their familiar toolkit and experiment with watercolor, colored pencils, and graphic films. Archigram's Michael Webb was (and presumably still is) a master of the airbrush. Watercolors by Zoe Zenghelis gave the rhetoric of Rem Koolhaas's *Delirious New York* (1978) an iconic visual image, adding mood, sensation, and concreteness to the written text.[8] Following on from the "Architecture of the École des Beaux-Arts" exhibition at the Museum of Modern Art in New York in 1976, the rendered elevation, realized in colored pencil on yellow tracing paper, became the iconic image of Postmodernism in architecture. John Hejduk discovered that the chemicals lingering on sepia prints (a common form of diazo printing, used to make a print that was itself transparent and could be used to print additional copies) partially dissolved the Prismacolor pencils he used, imparting a rich, waxy sheen to the colored areas. For my part, I remember painstakingly cutting out

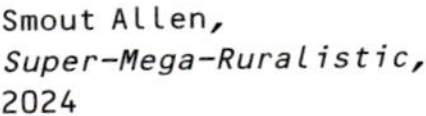

right: Model sketches aim to capture the fluid interactions within the scheme. These models articulate the shifting relationships between river and landscape, conveying both schematic structures and the dynamic systems at play.

opposite: Elevation showing the "Riverine Model Farm," cantilever barns and agricultural infrastructure on a raised landscape platform above floodplains and riparian woodland.

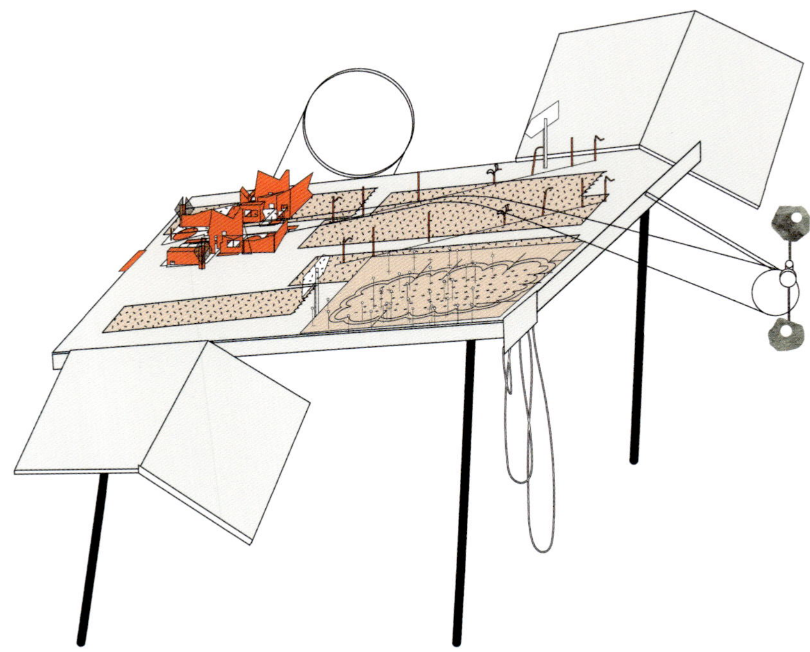

sheets of Pantone graphic film laid over line drawings, taking care to apply precisely the right amount of pressure on the number 11 X-Acto blade to trim the color without slicing through the underlying Mylar support.

This was the state of play in the late 1970s when master-printer John Nichols started working with architects. Printmaking offered his early clients (Michael Graves, Peter Eisenman, Steven Holl, and Thom Mayne among others) an expanded palette and a seamless integration of line and color. Silkscreen and lithography made possible a broad range of colors, rich gradations of transparency, and the possibility of incorporating found images: photographs, textures, dot-screens. Hence, with a few exceptions, the works exhibited in "The Sixth Somewhat Annual Meeting" at the A83 gallery (the successor to John Nichols Printmakers & Publishers) are not drawings; they are prints. This informal group (which is not really a group, they insist) worked closely with gallerists and printers Owen Nichols and Clare Syme, and were encouraged to experiment with the possibilities of silkscreen printing, a medium new to many of these architects.

I initially misread Smout Allen's project title Super-Mega-Ruralistic as "realistic," and Microsoft Word continues to correct the title each time I type it. I am pretty sure this is intentional, as the project is at once rural and real. Real, in the sense that it is a fully imagined and fully realized proposition, a story complete in itself, told through drawings.

The architects describe their proposal as a response to the "industrialized notion of landscapes as systems to be engineered and controlled, a concept rooted in the 'machine in the garden' narrative, exemplified by the Tennessee Valley Authority's 20th-century ambitions."[9] Jumping off from Leo Marx's *The Machine in the Garden* (1964),[10] an analysis of the anxious co-existence of machine and nature in 19th-century American painting and literature, they take on an iconic public work of the 20th century—one with vast resources and ambitions, situated at the cusp of modernity. Note that before the rural electrification made possible by the hydro-power of the Tennessee Valley Authority (TVA) dams, many Appalachian hamlets were still living under essentially pre-modern conditions. The TVA brought modern

improvements and jobs to the region, but it also submerged working farms and displaced countless families. Nearly a century later, Mark Smout and Laura Allen ask, what is the status of these landscapes, and what is the agency of architecture at the territorial scale as we move into the second quarter of the 21st century?

Just as contemporary ideas of forest stewardship have begun to question the consequences of fire-suppression, decades of flood-control policies are now suspect. The channeling of the Mississippi River has exacerbated flooding downriver, and destroyed the wetlands that were the natural protection from Gulf of Mexico storms. The progressive, Modernist ideology of nature as wild and unformed, waiting to be domesticated and controlled through large-scale technological intervention, is no longer sustainable. Ecologists now understand that periodic fires renew the forest, and flooding enriches the soil. Smout Allen's project embraces this new condition. They imagine large swaths of the Tennessee Valley as flooded, and invent new architectures, new patterns of land occupation, and new infrastructures to re-inhabit this territory.

SUPER-MEGA-RURALISTIC

For Smout Allen, constraints are opportunities, and
they have worked to invent and rework techniques of
representation. They have drawn the project at scales
ranging from 1:10,000 to 1:100, and they mix plan
drawings, axonometrics, and models

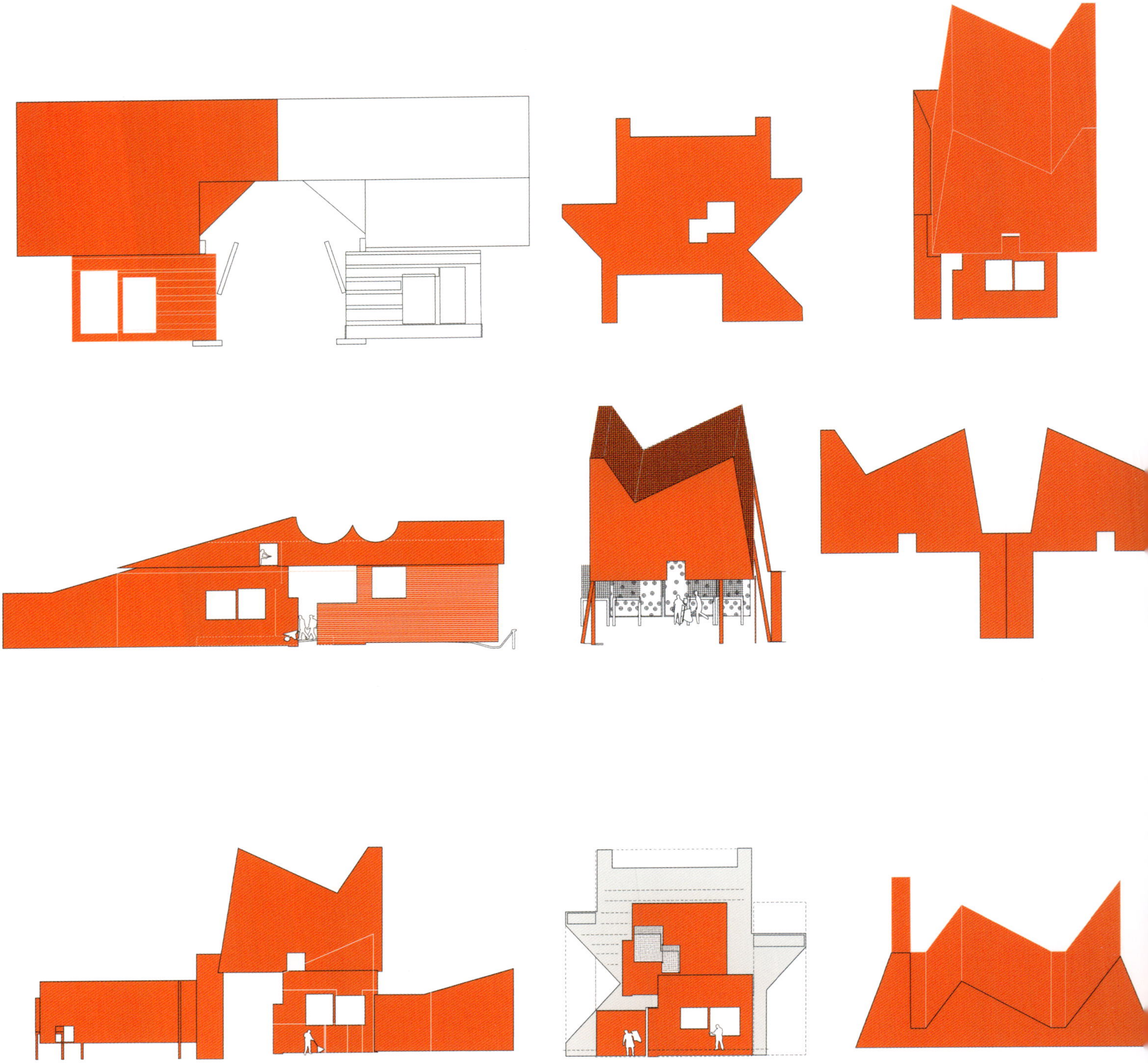

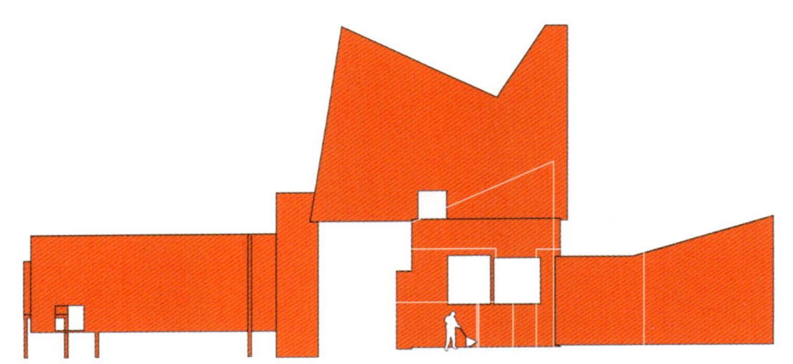

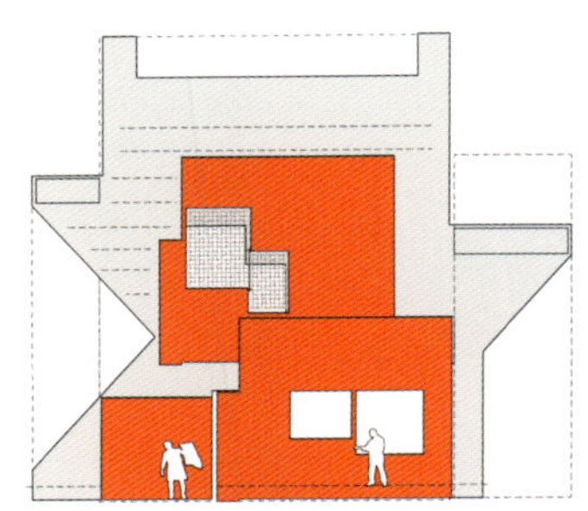

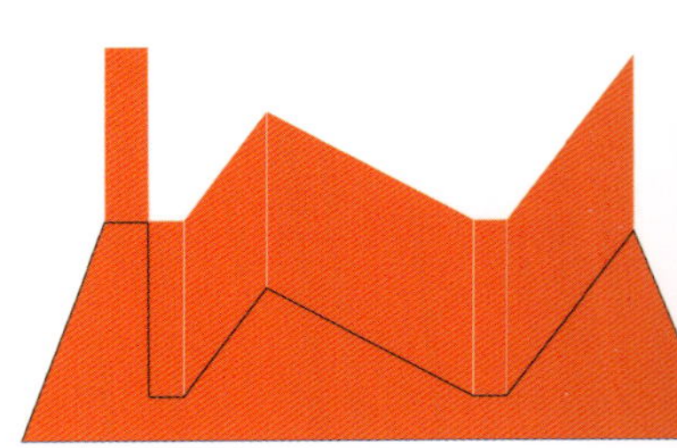

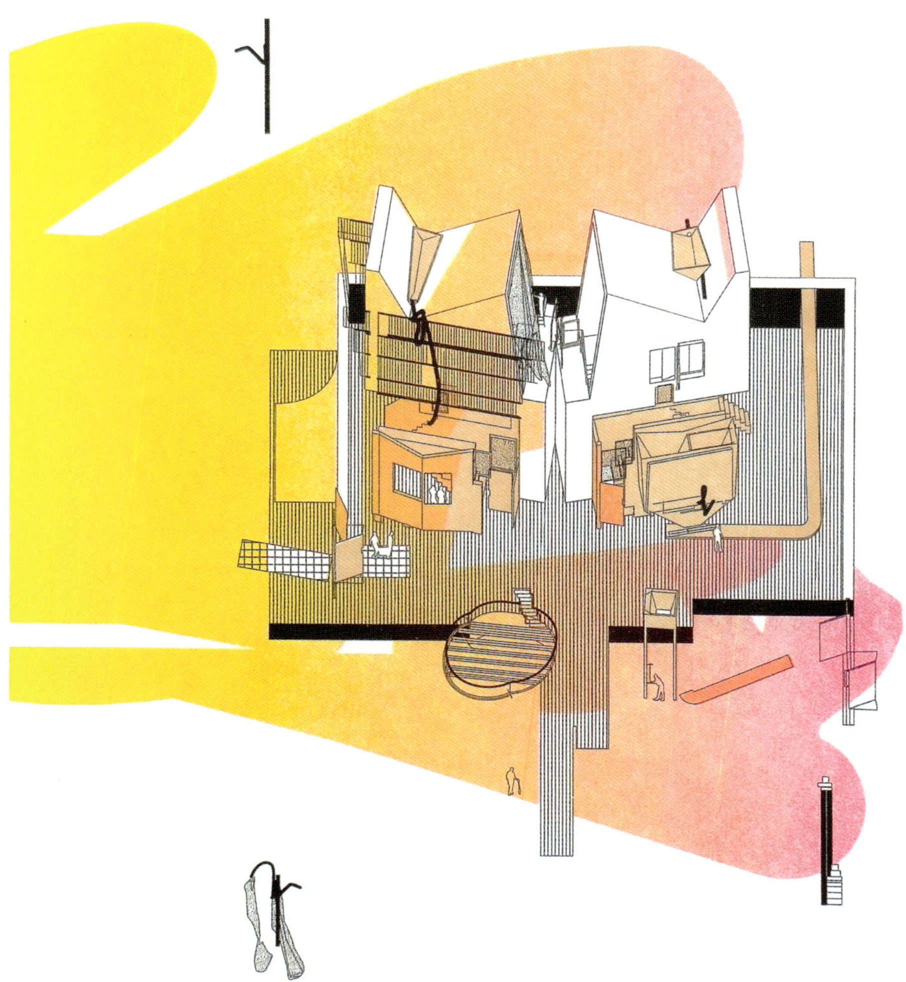

Smout Allen, *Super-Mega-Ruralistic*, 2024

opposite: Taking reference from vernacular cantilever barns, a hybrid barn design merges domestic and agricultural forms, with a raised crib providing shelter and direct connection to surrounding agricultural zones.

left: Riso print of a planometric drawing revealing the shared enclosures and technologies of both domestic and agricultural spaces, overlapping utility with dwelling. Produced for *Records of the Sixth Somewhat Annual Meeting*, exhibition folio, A83 gallery, New York (2025).

Theirs is also a project that complicates the narrative of a pastoral countryside and an urbanized metropolis. Modern technology is everywhere in the rural landscape today, from roadways and cars, electrical grids, and mechanized agriculture, to invisible networks of communication. The model farms that Smout Allen imagine in this new landscape are surrounded by greenhouses for research and food production that flood the night landscape with an eerie yellow light. This is less the familiar idea that "all nature is constructed nature" than it is a pervasive mixing of natural and artificial in which each concept is impossible to imagine without the other—that perhaps over-used notion of the Anthropocene, here given a very precise expression.

Landscape architects have struggled to adapt tools of representation inherited from architecture—techniques that developed over centuries to describe freestanding buildings. For Smout Allen, constraints are opportunities, and they have worked to invent and rework techniques of representation. They have drawn the project at scales ranging from 1:10,000 to 1:100, and they mix plan drawings, axonometrics, and models. They know that just as architectural representation works through abstraction, landscape is best alluded to, rather than represented literally. In their drawings, dashed-line arrays suggest at once furrowed fields and the dappled light of the forest, cut off in ways that suggest an extent far beyond the limit of the paper.

Geometry textbooks tell us that a line has no thickness, only length: a vector drawn between two points, the pencil stroke nothing more than a compromise to notate the abstract geometric idea. "Line-weight" is, in fact, an oxymoron. And strictly speaking, in a silkscreen there are no lines, only attenuated strips of black. Mad filaments, "thin strings of hue," as William Gass has put it.[11]

Laura Allen has spoken of needing to extensively rework their drawings to accommodate the constraints of the screenprint, with the consequence that their lines now have a bold, punchy quality. These lines (which may no longer be lines) are not simply a delicate scaffolding delineating areas of color, but an equal protagonist, with an equivalent graphic presence to the rich colors in the drawings and prints.

In the screenprint made for the folio produced in association with the A83 exhibition, for example, an irregularly shaped swath of color floods in from the left, vibrant yellow shading to pink, like a blushing teenager. Water? Field? Sand blown in from some distant beach? Impossible to tell. Simultaneously ground and figure, this patch of color weaves the drawn architecture onto the page, and by suggestion, the site. And then there is that strange, worm-like squiggle defacing the elevation of the barn, that could be water from a scupper, or an errant vine, but probably isn't.

Simply another mark, which collapses the drawing onto the picture plane, at precisely the moment it wants to suggest depth and three-dimensional space. The architecture is at once of the land and apart from the land, just as the drawing is a representation of the project and at the same time a collection of marks on paper.

More so than other work in the exhibition, Smout Allen's drawings invite translation into imagined buildings and landscapes—there are even scale figures. The most recognizable structure in the drawings is a working barn, derived from the vernacular architecture of East Tennessee. There is an (intentionally) awkward set to the barn in their drawings, as if it has shifted off its foundation, a not unlikely scenario given the imagined flood: a nuanced suggestion of the precarity of occupying the land under contemporary conditions of climate change, a crisis that promises to disrupt the very ground of the habitable planet.

Smout Allen simultaneously accept and complicate the conventions of architectural representation. They embrace the double condition of architectural drawing as at once a working tool of design, a story told about a future to come, and at the same time, an autonomous work, intelligible on its own terms, and in dialogue with other drawings, other histories. ⅅ

The architecture is at once of the land and apart from the land, just as the drawing is a representation of the project and at the same time a collection of marks on paper

Smout Allen, *Super-Mega-Ruralistic,* 2024

Three screenprints for "The Sixth Somewhat Annual Meeting" exhibition at the A83 gallery, New York, 2025. The drawings incorporate an additional split-fountain screen to evoke the shifting movement of light across the landscape and industrialized agricultural territories.

Notes

1. William Gass, *On Being Blue: A Philosophical Inquiry* [1976], New York Review Books (New York), 2014, p. 74.
2. Zoe Zenghelis, "Roosevelt Island," Drawing Matter, February 17, 2019: https://drawingmatter.org/roosevelt-island/.
3. Immanuel Kant, "Critique of Aesthetic Judgment," in *The Critique of Judgment* [1790], tr. James Creed Meredith, Clarendon Press (Oxford), 1911, p. 225.
4. Quoted in Edward S. King, "Ingres as Classicist," *The Journal of the Walters Art Gallery*, 5, 1942, p. 98.
5. Eugène Delacroix, undated entry, 1852, *The Journal of Eugène Delacroix*, tr. Lucy Norton, Phaidon Press (London), 1995, p. 177.
6. Leon Battista Alberti, *On the Art of Building in Ten Books*, tr. Joseph Rykwert et al., MIT Press (Cambridge, MA), 1991, p. 3.
7. Le Corbusier, *The Decorative Art of Today* [1925], MIT Press (Cambridge, MA), 1987, p. 188.
8. Rem Koolhaas, *Delirious New York: A Retroactive Manifesto for Manhattan*, Oxford University Press (New York), 1978.
9. Smout Allen, unpublished project description, personal communication to the author.
10. Leo Marx, *The Machine in the Garden: Technology and the Pastoral Ideal in America*, Oxford University Press (New York), 1964.
11. Gass, *On Being Blue,* p. 74.

Adam Dayem

ANGELS in the ARCHITECTURE

MYSTERIES OF CONTEXT AND DURATION

Creative inspiration can strike at any time and across time through acts of memory. Photography can momentarily stop a small aspect of time.

Adam Dayem, an architect and educator based in Brooklyn, New York, explores the work of London architect Shaun Murray who over the years has developed his own language of architecture and its relationship to context. The "Ineffaceable Illuminations" series, developed with the gallerists of A83, is a kind of psycho-geographic journey across familiar landscapes and places inspired by a dog walking field and 15 years of photographic recordings of such treks, synthesised together, to create Murray's layered works.

Shaun Murray,
Sixth Street Revisited,
"Ineffaceable Illuminations" series,
A83 gallery,
New York,
2025

top: The drawing is composed of superimposed layers of transparent acetate. The separate layers are seen here during the process of being printed at A83.

Shaun Murray,
Sixth Street Revisited,
"Ineffaceable Illuminations" series,
2025

bottom: Superimposed layers of acetate printed with colored forms of varying transparency, informed by sketches based on photos taken during ritual walks through a field in Cumbria, Northwest England.

Shaun Murray,
Sixth Street Revisited,
"Ineffaceable
Illuminations" series,
"The Sixth Somewhat
Annual Meeting"
exhibition," A83
gallery,
New York,
2025

The drawing was mounted
on a transparent background
for the exhibition. The
parallax effect between the
drawing floating in space
and shadows projected
on the wall behind it
destabilized readings of the
drawing as viewers moved
around it.

Shaun Murray's drawing *Sixth Street Revisited* (2025), part of his "Ineffaceable Illuminations" series, connects rational and intuitive worlds. This is what many architectural drawings do; they deal with parts of the world that are measurable and quantifiable—the dimensions of a building site or the weight of materials, for example—yet they do not seek to quantify everything that falls into their purview. They remain open to imaginative interpretation. So critical in discussing Murray's work is not simply the fact that it bridges between rational and intuitive, qualitative and quantitative, knowable and unknowable, but rather how specifically his drawing holds these tensions, which reveals important aspects of his approach, and how his intentions produce meaning for viewers.

Great works of art often deal with the tension between rational and intuitive worlds. For example, in 1999 David Lynch, who was famously reluctant to discuss the meaning of his movies in public or otherwise, gave an in-depth interview with the filmmaker Mark Cousins for the BBC TV series *Scene by Scene*.[1] At one point in the interview, Cousins points out to Lynch that there are often angels in his films. Lynch initially demurs, seemingly not wanting to touch the topic of angels, but Cousins cites specific examples.

> Cousins: "You don't literally believe in angels?"
> Lynch: "Oh yeah."
> Cousins: "No you don't, do you?"
> Lynch: "Yeah."

Cousins seems incredulous and presses on:

> "You don't literally mean top of the Christmas tree type thing?"

And Lynch finally responds:

> "There are many things I think that are out there that we don't know about, but sometimes you get certain feelings."

In this exchange, Lynch encounters the tension between rational and intuitive worlds, between the knowable and the unknowable. The prevailing way of seeing the world in Western philosophy and culture tries to explain away things we deeply understand to be true but cannot rationalize. Rather than trying to rationalize Murray's drawings, one has to enter them as one would enter a David Lynch film—one has to leave a space for angels to exist.

Adam Dayem,
Photographic series,
SoHo, New York,
2025

Views of art galleries, including A83, taken from the streets of the SoHo neighborhood of Manhattan. These views show the wider context in which Murray intended *Sixth Street Revisited* to be experienced.

Specific Sites

Murray created *Sixth Street Revisited* as a site-specific installation for "The Sixth Somewhat Annual Meeting" exhibition at the A83 gallery and printmaking studio in the SoHo district of Manhattan, New York. The drawing was produced on-site at A83 as a series of layered acetate sheets onto which colors and shapes of varying levels of transparency were printed. Because it was made as a screenprint, the drawing is unique within Murray's body of work, but the process of screenprinting does reflect his typical way of working, which is to airbrush transparent, colored shapes onto acetate. The most significant difference between this drawing and his others is that it was mounted floating in space, so the transparency of the acetate remained perceptible. One could see through the background of the drawing to its shadow projected onto the wall behind. More typically in Murray's work, contextual information such as a site photograph is placed behind the layers of transparent acetate, an example of which can be seen in *The Pendulum* (2021), also part of his "Ineffaceable Illuminations" series. Murray's drawings are always contextual, and in the case of *Sixth Street Revisited* the context was the space of the gallery itself and its relationship to the city, including other art galleries in the surrounding neighborhood.

As a site-specific installation in relation to its context, the drawing intentionally forces its viewers to deal with time. For Murray, it is important that the viewer has made the trip to Lower Manhattan, entered the gallery, and moved around the drawing, experiencing how the shadow projected on the wall shifts in relation to it. This is an antidote to the immediacy of viewing drawings on Instagram or even printed in books or magazines. The viewer must slow down, enter the context of the drawing, and experience it over time. This way of experiencing a work, over time and in context, is of course very familiar to architects as it is the only way buildings are truly experienced. But for Murray, notions of time and context are more complex. We are all time-travelers in a way, he says,[2] and time travel is deeply embedded in his drawings.

Shaun Murray,
The Pendulum,
"Ineffaceable
Illuminations" series,
2021

Airbrushed acetate layers superimposed over a photograph of the Battersea Bridge spanning the River Thames in London. In this drawing, the photograph is the context in which the drawing operates.

Shaun Murray,
Sketching series,
2025

A series of ritual sketches based on
the photographs taken of the field in
Cumbria. The sketches were used to
edit, sense, and respond to the field as a
site that is both physical and imaginary.
They ultimately informed the individual
layers and the relationships between
them in Sixth Street Revisited.

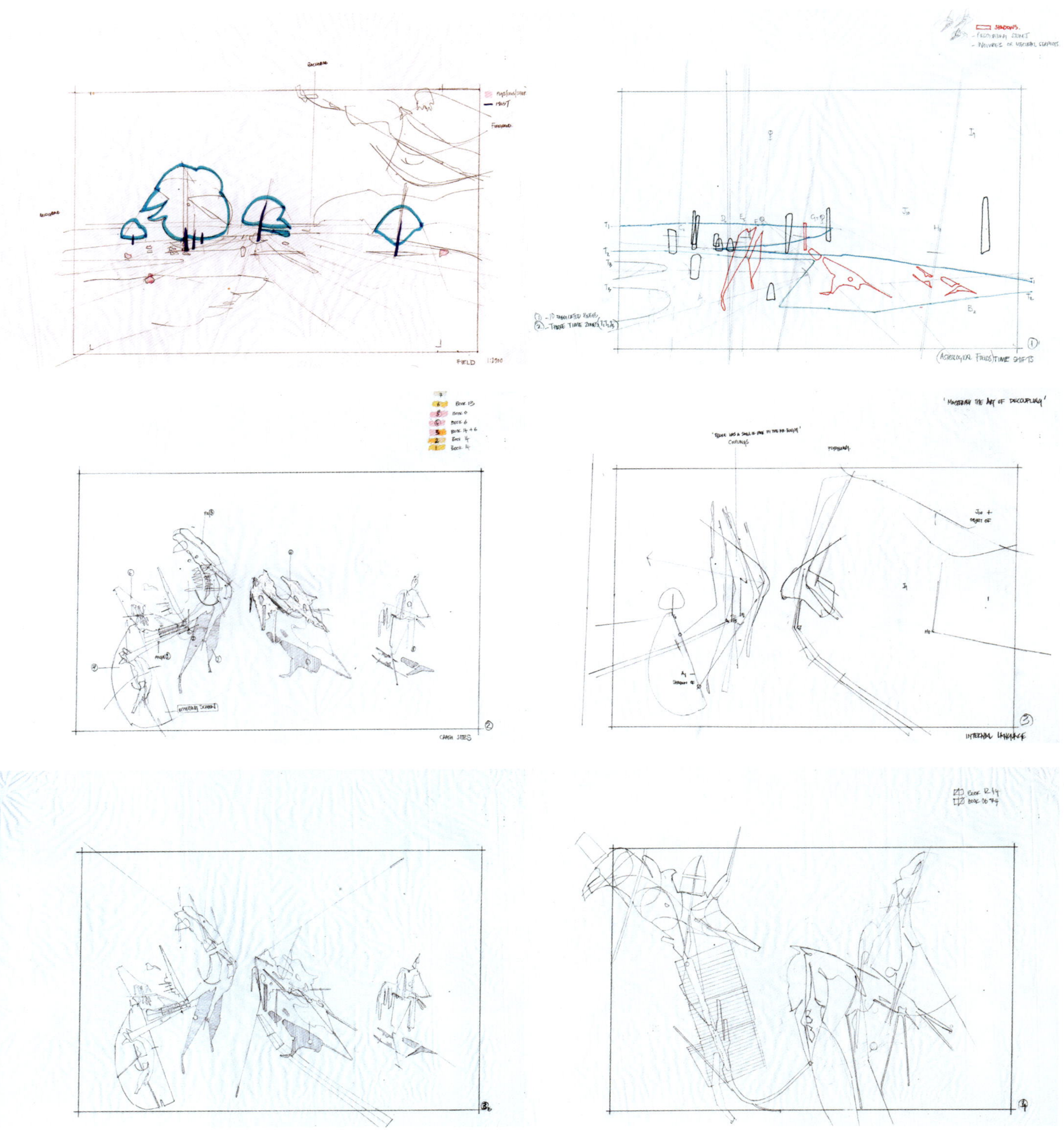

Time Traveling

Sixth Street Revisited emerged from a fascination with American architect Thom Mayne's *6th Street Residence* (1987–92) drawing series. Murray is interested in Mayne's drawings not as static images or form, but as "interlocking elements of somebody's routine in designing their own home."[3] Routines, particularly in a domestic setting, operate partly in the past through memory, and partly in the present. They are embedded in the body as the past is continually recapitulated and brought forward into the present through habit. Routines are not intellectualized or even completely conscious activities. Murray has introduced his own routine to the drawing process—walks in a field in Cumbria, Northwest England, with his mother and sister. Over a period of 15 years, he took a series of photographs in the field. He saw parts of the scenery in the photographs, such as the trees, working as interlocking elements that constructed an imaginary field occupied in space and time. He then introduced another routine—sketching—and made a series of pencil drawings of these elements, translating them into the abstract shapes that eventually informed the colored shapes printed on layers of acetate in the final *Sixth Street Revisited* drawing.

In some respects, Murray uses interlocking elements extracted from his photographs in a similar manner to how Mayne used them to build up his *Sixth Street House* drawings. In both cases, the elements activate fields that are occupied in time and space. They both use a unique system of architectural notation, but in completely different ways. Mayne's drawings reinterpret spatial conventions of architecture by creating unexpected or paradoxical combinations of objects within spaces. They deploy known conventions of architectural notation in unusual ways: slicing diagonally rather than rectilinearly, juxtaposing orthographic and isometric projections rather than keeping them separate, and superimposing shadows projected from different directions, to name a few examples. The drawings, while they have a life of their own, are intended to lead to a building, the Sixth Street House itself, and then eventually to a lineage of buildings produced by Mayne's architectural firm Morphosis.

Shaun Murray,
Photographic series,
Dalton-in-Furness,
Cumbria, England,
2010-25

A selection of photographs from a larger series taken over a period of 15 years, in different seasons, on ritual walks through a field in Cumbria.

Shaun Murray,
*Tactile Planchette on the
field cartographies at Mill
Brow in Dalton-in-Furness,*
2025

The physical clay model overlaid
on the acetate drawing. Physical
models are conceived by Murray
as tactile devices for reading and
interpreting his drawings.

If Mayne is an artist of space, then Murray is an artist of time.[4] If Mayne treats the conventions of architectural notation as constructed, then Murray treats them as under construction. If Mayne ultimately sees drawing as a way of constructing a building, and all the determined stability that requires, then Murray sees it as constructing a way of thinking that does not produce determined outcomes. Because Murray's drawings do not lead up to a final building, they are free to loop the timeline of designing and building architecture back on itself, reconstructing what has already been constructed again and again. The American philosopher David Lewis's essay "The Paradoxes of Time Travel" (1976), which Murray cites as an influence, discusses causal loops in which knowledge from the future travels back to influence the past, which in turn influences the future, so that the initial production of that knowledge becomes utterly unknown.[5] Because of the fluidity with which Murray thinks about time, the origin of knowledge in his drawings is similarly mysterious. In writing about Murray's work, the British philosopher Nick Land discusses how different points in time can influence each other to unlock new ways of reimagining the built world so fundamental that our known world begins to feel rather precarious.[6]

Does one read all this time traveling in Murray's drawings at first glance? Most, if not all, casual viewers likely do not. An initial surface reading of *Sixth Street Revisited* reveals a beautiful composition of fields of superimposed color, transparency, and reflectivity. In the larger context of his work, Murray deals with the need for his cryptic fields of time and context to be accompanied by an interpretive device, which comes in the form of physical models. He describes the drawings as designing the world, and the physical models as interacting with the world. The models are readers of the drawings; they are the three-dimensional fragments of the drawing one touches while reading it. He heightens the mystery of the relationship between his models and drawings by comparing the models to planchettes or Ouija boards—devices meant to communicate with entities such as dead relatives, existing outside the known, rational world. Models, such as *Tactile Planchette on the field cartographies at Mill Brow in Dalton-in-Furness* (2025), therefore offer no known or rational interpretation of the drawings; they can only be used to interact intuitively with them.

Durational Drawings

While it may be impossible for most viewers to access the intellectual context needed to interpret the *Sixth Street Revisited* drawing at all the levels at which Murray is working, by conceiving it as a site-specific installation for a gallery show of architectural drawings he required the viewer to take the time to slow down and consider what the drawing means in terms of its relation to making and thinking about space. Experiencing the drawing in the gallery is an experience in time and space. Or to be more precise it is an experience that has "duration," in the sense that the French philosopher Henri Bergson described it.

For Bergson, duration is different from time: "When we speak of time, we generally think of a homogeneous medium in which our conscious states are ranged alongside one another as in space, so as to form a discrete multiplicity."[7] Whether dealing with discrete elements in space, or conscious states that come one after the other, Bergson argues that the perception of these multiplicities has to be in space. They are "quantitative" multiplicities that need spatial separation from one another to be perceptible. Duration, on the other hand, deals with heterogeneity, simultaneity, and interpenetration. For example, Bergson describes how sympathy unfolds in duration. In order to feel sympathy, one has to feel a number of things at the same time: the pain of the suffering of others, the desire to help alleviate pain, and the superiority that results from the awareness of one's ability to help.[8] Taken separately, each of these states has a completely different meaning; only when they are overlaid on each other and experienced simultaneously as heterogeneous, interpenetrating layers does one feel sympathy. This, for Bergson, is a "qualitative" multiplicity. It is inexpressible. It is experienced immediately without mediating signs or symbols. It is experienced intuitively without being rationalized.

This is how Murray's drawings should be experienced—as duration and as qualitative multiplicities. It is not necessary for the viewer to comprehend the process of making the drawings or to intellectualize the outcomes, because they are meant to be experienced durationally, which is to say they are meant to be experienced intuitively. Reading the drawings takes a certain amount of openness to the unknown and a willingness to let go of disciplinary training that encourages us to rationalize drawing, no matter how abstract, as progression toward building. We cannot fall into the rationalization trap as Cousins does when pressing Lynch about his beliefs. We must be willing to leave space for angels in Murray's drawings. And when this is done, his work reveals a completely different world for architectural representation, one that exists outside of time, in pure duration. In duration we are able to understand the world not as a succession of events, but as heterogeneous layers that must be experienced simultaneously through intuition. This offers a glimpse into a radically different future for the built world, and given the precariousness of our present, radical change may be coming whether we like it or not. ⌂

Notes

1. *Scene by Scene*, "David Lynch," YouTube video, November 28, 1999: www.youtube.com/watch?v=d0a1IIY7b1E.
2. In conversation with the author, February 24, 2025.
3. Ibid.
4. Nick Land, "Introductions to the Afterlife," *Design Ecologies*, 2 (1), 2012, p. 17.
5. David Lewis, "The Paradoxes of Time Travel," *American Philosophical Quarterly*, April 1976, p. 148.
6. Land, "Introductions to the Afterlife," p. 25.
7. Henri Bergson, *Time and Free Will: An Essay on the Immediate Data of Consciousness* [1910], tr. F.L. Pogson, Kessinger Publishing Company (Whitefish, MT), 2014, pp. 59–60.
8. Bergson, *Time and Free Will*, pp. 17–8.

Jimenez Lai

THE FLATNESS OF DEPTH

VANISHING POINTS AND DULLING TONES

FACULTY MEMBER AT THE UNIVERSITY OF SOUTHERN CALIFORNIA SCHOOL OF ARCHITECTURE AND FOUNDER OF BUREAU SPECTACULAR, **JIMENEZ LAI**, WRITING ON THE WORK OF ARCHITECT AND ARTIST OWEN NICHOLS, CONCERNS HIMSELF WITH ISSUES OF FLATNESS AND REDUCING TONAL COLOR AS A MEANS OF FURTHER FLATTENING VISUAL DEPTH. NICHOLS ALIGHTS ON A MICHAEL GRAVES IMAGE IN HIS COLLECTION AND THE WOODBLOCKS THAT CREATED IT. NICHOLS'S NEW WORK BREATHES NEW LIFE INTO THE OLDER WORK OF GRAVES AND ADDS TO ITS GENEALOGY.

Owen Nichols,
Icky,
2025

Owen Nichols reinterpreted Michael Graves's drawing, *Domestic Landscape,* as a 2.5-D drawdel. Rendered shadows are mixed with physical shadows, constructing a depth within an otherwise flat drawing.

Flatness, a conceptual platform from which orthographic projections allow architects to translate 2D drawings into 3D volumes, is more than just a working format. Flatness, as a means to abstract, transforms physical reality into objectively measurable planes that reflect the cultural concerns of the day. In the exhibition "The Sixth Somewhat Annual Meeting" at the New York gallery A83, Owen Nichols constructed a drawdel titled *Icky* (2025)—a 2.5-D object that is halfway between a drawing and a model—to reinterpret Michael Graves's *Domestic Landscape*, a 1984 woodblock print held in the John Nichols Printmakers and Publishers Collection. Owen Nichols, master printmaker, teacher, and curator at the A83 gallery, grew up around the late great architect and Princeton University professor Michael Graves. According to Nichols, Graves's drawings were characteristically flat, rarely employing perspective projection. Nichols, who was close to Graves, has theorized that this approach was influenced by Graves's amblyopia, a medical condition colloquially known as "lazy eye," which may have affected his depth perception. As a result, his spaces—while rendered primarily in two dimensions—carry a strong spatial implication, especially in his planimetric compositions. However, through the drawdel of Nichols, there is more to the flatness of Graves. Between Graves and Nichols, one can also find traces of the eras they belong to: techniques within Postmodernism, and a newer contemporary sensibility. This translation is a conversation between Graves and Nichols, as they renegotiate flatness in two ways: a flat projection of a subject, a dulling of the tone. Both forms of flatness produced a reflective depth.

A Flat Projection of a Subject

In the original *Domestic Landscape* and *Alternative Landscape* by Michael Graves, there is a conceptual conundrum: while both drawings appear to be elevation obliques, both also contain vanishing points. The conflict here is that it is illogical for an orthographic projection to also be a perspectival drawing, unless a perspective begins only beyond a cutting plane. In both of Graves's drawings, foreshortening is mixed into an otherwise completely flat drawing. What is the big deal? one might ask. The issue here is that a vanishing point confirms the presence of a subject looking, mixed into an orthographic projection that conveys total objectivity.

Art historian and professor Yve-Alain Bois, in his seminal 1981 essay "Metamorphosis of Axonometry," distinguished the perspectival drawing from the axonometric drawing by examining the status of the vanishing point. A vanishing point, which is the focal infinity bounded by the lens length of a human eye, indicates the presence of a viewing person—a subjective sensorial drawing.[1] Conversely, the axonometric drawing documents an objectively quantitative environment, lacking the presence of a subject. Both drawings are three-dimensional, although the perspective can be metrically constructed, but only the axonometric is measurable with a ruler in its flatness.

For Graves, the flattening and deepening happened simultaneously. As the orthographic projection and perspectival drawing coexist, Graves acknowledges the coexistence of the lack of a subject through the orthographic conventions, and the presence of a viewer for the drawing itself. Whereas most working drawings flatten faces to communicate dimensions and proportions, the purpose of both *Domestic Landscape* and *Alternative Landscape* is to engage an audience that treats the drawings as viewing objects in themselves.

Michael Graves,
Domestic Landscape,
1984

Michael Graves's window landscape drawing, *Domestic Landscape,* where the ambiguity of inside or outside is blurred. Originally produced for an exhibition, Intuition and the Block Print, at John Nichols's gallery, curated by J. Nebraska Gifford.

The fabrication process of the original *Domestic Landscape* and *Alternative Landscape* is key to how Owen Nichols eventually reconstructed his translation piece. The Japanese woodblock printers used a layered stenciling technique, which deconstructed the drawing surfaces into flat color planes. According to Nichols: In 1984, Japanese publisher RYU commissioned Michael Graves to create two print editions using traditional Japanese woodblock techniques. For *Alternative Landscape*, Graves had recently completed a wall mural and submitted a photograph as reference. For *Domestic Landscape*, he provided an original drawing, which was subsequently reproduced as a woodblock print.

Like a shadow-puppet theater, *Icky* disassembles Graves's drawing into layers of flat planes, individual characters in a frame. Nichols's technique is similar to the logic of the Japanese woodblock printing, where each stencil is separated layer by layer. Physically cutting out flat surfaces, and letting physical depth become the image, was the process from which Owen Nichols translated Graves's work. Similar to the logic of stenciling, each 2D cutout was staged like a diorama. Nichols hand drew shades onto each layer; this drawdel graduates *Domestic Landscape* from an architectural drawing into a theatrical scene with objecthood.

Yet, in 2025, the primary method of dissemination is the photography shared on social media. Nichols constructs something three-dimensional out of a two-dimensional drawing, only for the image to be widely circulated in two-dimensions again. In this case, while the lens length of a camera inherently makes the image a perspectival one, the vast majority of viewing subjects encounter the Nichols translation either on a screen, or as a print. Both cases are a flattening experience. The print is flat, and the screen is flat—but the eyeballs of the audience function as many new vanishing points, fragmenting the medium into multiple subjectivities.

Owen Nichols,
Icky,
2025

Owen Nichols, with former collaborator Mark Acciari, worked to cut out fragments of Michael Graves's *Domestic Landscape*. This photograph captures a moment in the process of identifying the flat components with rendered shadows, but also attains physical shadows.

Ito Mokuhan,
Cherry woodblock plate of
Domestic Landscape,
at Mokuhan Printers,
Tokyo,
1984

A double-sided woodblock from the
production of *Domestic Landscape* by
Michael Graves, hand carved by Ito
Mokuhan Printers, Japan.

A Dulling of the Tone

Flatness can also be about color. Flatness is not only about a two-dimensional planar condition: the word "flat" is also often used chromatically, to mean a pastel or desaturated tone. What is the connotation of dulling out an otherwise saturated color, and what message does it send? In the case of Michael Graves, both *Domestic Landscape* and *Alternative Landscape* contain flat colors. Furthermore, the color and materiality of the *Portland Building* (1982) indicates that the off-primary is even present in his built work. Flatness, in terms of color, is almost a declarative statement in opposition to the colors of abstraction.

Just over 70 years prior, the *De Stijl Manifesto* (1918)[2] was published by Dutch painter, writer, and architect Theo van Doesburg and his collaborators, including Piet Mondrian, Antony Kok, Robert van't Hoff, and others. The abolition of "natural form," an opposition to "traditions, dogmas and the domination of the individual," or a "new consciousness of time" are just some of the key principles postulated by the group. Members of De Stijl stated something very deterministic and definitive in their collective pursuit. In fact, this idea of a new consciousness desires something elemental, something universal: a singular grand narrative—a key feature of what we know now as Modernism.

Ito Mokuhan proofing *Domestic
Landscape* with Redlines at
Mokuhan Printers,
Tokyo,
1984

Ito Mokuhan compares the first
proofing with the notes and redlines
to the final edition printing of Michael
Graves's *Domestic Landscape.*

Indeed, the full intensity and the elemental quality of the color is the aesthetics of an absolute determinism, a visual signifier that captured the spirit of Modernism. The members of De Stijl expressed their ideals with orthogonal Cartesian grids, but also with primary colors. Red, blue, yellow, black, and white are the only colors to turn a page from the complications of history, and start anew in abstract ways. The colors of this era, including those of Fauvism, Constructivism, Suprematism, Nouveau Réalisme, and others, are each pure, full, elemental, saturated, and bright. Such is the passion one feels when the First World War destroys every notion of the past, and a red as true as blood is the only reliable sense of absolute. In architecture, the rationalism of geometries and the sterility of materiality also contributed to the idea that some forms and functions were the one true international style.

By Graves's generation, however, the paradigm had been shifting. Questions about the status of Modernism emerged in many other fields, including philosophy, cinema, art, literature, and eventually architecture. Charles Jencks, one of the most consequential figures in the definition of Postmodernism in architecture, wrote in his 1992 publication *The Post-Modern Reader*:

"The argument has crystallised into two philosophies— what I and many others call Neo- and Post-Modernism— both of which share the notion that the modern world is coming to an end, and that something new must replace it. They differ over whether the previous world view should be taken to an extreme and made more radical, or synthesised with other approaches at a higher level."[3]

Michael Graves, a key figure who took on the end of the "previous world" through his work and teaching, went on to help define Postmodernism in architecture. In *Domestic Landscape* and *Alternative Landscape*, as a matter of chromatic counterpoint, he departs from the fully saturated or primary color schemes of Modernism. In opposition to the pureness of red, yellow, or blue, Graves introduced shades of contaminated, muted, worn, and seasoned colors to contest the singular grand narrative. Irony, a key rhetorical device to cast a sense of skepticism and relativism, was the central ingredient in Postmodern discourse. In place of the absolute sincerity of Modernism, the flatness of the color is a symbolic point of departure.

Michael Graves,
Alternative Landscape,
1984

opposite: Michael Graves's window
landscape drawing, *Alternative
Landscape*, where the ambiguity of
inside or outside is blurred. Originally
produced for an exhibition, "Intuition
and the Block Print," at John Nichols's
gallery, curated by J. Nebraska Gifford.

Michael Graves,
Window Landscape,
New York,
1988

below: John Nichols produced a flat
screenprint of Michael Graves's window
landscape drawing. In this case,
Window Landscape.

IN OPPOSITION TO THE PURENESS OF RED, YELLOW, OR BLUE, GRAVE
INTRODUCED SHADES OF CONTAMINATED, MUTED, WORN, AND
SEASONED COLORS TO CONTEST THE SINGULAR GRAND NARRATIVE

below: Owen Nichols translated the *Icky* drawdel, re-flattening the rendered and physical shadows into a two-dimensional representation.

opposite: Owen Nichols reinterpreted Michael Graves's *Domestic Landscape* as a 2.5-D drawdel. Rendered shadows are mixed with physical shadows, constructing a depth within an otherwise flat drawing. This image shows *Icky* in the context of the group exhibition "The Sixth Somewhat Annual Meeting" held at A83 gallery in SoHo, NY, in 2025.

However, the translation by Owen Nichols tells a different story of the times. The gradients of white, as well as the hand-drawn shading, both contain a near-norm sensibility and reflect a different cultural moment. In 2017, theorists Robin van den Akker, Alison Gibbons, and Timotheus Vermeulen co-edited *Metamodernism*,[4] a collection of essays about historicity, affect, and depth after postmodernism. Van den Akker, Gibbons, and Vermeulen are cultural theorists and contemporary philosophers who have been observing the detailed nuances of the post-postmodern era of the 2010s. Many contributors to this book were asking a similar question about a new relationship with referentiality, originality, irony, and sincerity. From the post-irony of the late author and professor David Foster Wallace to the indifference of architect and professor Michael Meredith, a root of this cultural moment can be traced to the New Sincerity Movement:

> "What is The New Sincerity? Think of it as irony and sincerity combined like Voltron, to form a new movement of astonishing power. Or think of it as the absence of irony and sincerity, where less is (obviously) more."[5]

Whereas irony was a device to subvert Modernism, in Nichols's generation irony is but a reflex and a tone of voice. This new version of the elemental, minimal, or normal is a sincere desire to opt out of the obviously cool. Aesthetically, Nichols's *Icky* has more in common with the minimalism from a century ago, yet has the rhetorical intelligence of Graves's era. Nichols's off-white translation with the low relief, textured shadows against the physical shadows, in juxtaposition to Graves's flat-color original, display the tonal difference of their respective cultural moments.

Nichols's drawdel is a set without a character. Or, perhaps the backdrop itself is the character of a story that acknowledges the viewer as the subject. Flatness is the fourth wall that Michael Graves consistently broke. Graves, in Nichols's recount, was always an author who wrote, drew, and built with a knowing nod to an informed audience. In both *Domestic Landscape* and *Alternative Landscape*, there is a frame within the frame. Compositionally, a perspectival drawing is able to take place inside of the frame of an orthographic elevation. Graves placed vanishing points within a canvas frame and a window frame, as though he knew the distance the audience would have to the art object would negate the status of the drawing as an architectural object—the type of flat object that has a reflective depth. Yet, the power of this posthumous conversation between Graves and Nichols also aptly captured the paradigm shifts of their times, whether a skepticism of the sincerity of Modernism, or an oscillation of a post-irony sincerity in the 21st century. In an era of disposable digital content, printed flat leaflets are the most inexpensive but consequential political artifacts. ⌀

Notes

1. Yve-Alain Bois, "Metamorphosis of Axonometry," Daidalos (no. 1), 1981.
2. De Stijl, volume 2, novembre 1918–octobre 1919.
3. Charles Jencks, *The Post-Modern Reader*, Academy Editions, 1992.
4. Robin van den Akker, Alison Gibbons, and Timotheus Vermeulen (eds), *Metamodernism: Historicity, Affect and Depth After Postmodernism*, Rowman & Littlefield Publishers (London), 2017.
5. Jesse Thorn, "Manifesto for New Sincerity," 2006. www.maximumfun.org/blog/2006/02/manifesto-for-new-sincerity.html.

IV
4
4
CALCULATION SHEET

Peter J. Baldwin

Architectural Alchemy
Concerning the Coming of Venus

In a text that is as full of allusions as Δ Editor's Neil Spiller's drawings, English architect and teacher **Peter J. Baldwin** explores a small portion of Spiller's recent project *Halcyon Daze-Astonishing Panoramas* (2024). The piece he focuses on is the *Pluck's Gutter Mannequin Shop*, the initial inspiration for which was three prints by American architect Anthony Ames held in the A83 archive in New York. Once laced with uncanny surrealism, 'Pataphysical swerves, and a magical realist narrative, this heady concoction blossoms into a series of architectural scenarios that are a microcosm of the wider *Halcyon Daze* project.

Neil Spiller,
Front Façade, Pluck's Gutter Mannequin Shop, "Halcyon Daze,
Astonishing Panoramas" series,
2024

Primarily a reference to Marcel Duchamp's *The Bride Stripped Bare by Her Bachelors, Even (The Large Glass)* (1915–23), although vertically, rather than horizontally, bisected. The sinister side of the façade reveals a feminine form, symbolizing art, creativity, and the cycles of the natural world. On its dexter, Spiller's *Dorian Gray Column* (1984), composed of classical architectural orders, associated with technology as physical fulfillment. The unity of the façade represents the opposing aspects of architectural meaning embodied in the tension of logic and lust.

Anthony Ames,
Egg, Angel, and *Cornice,*
1987

Formed of a series of appropriated purist
objects and Modernist vistas, Ames's works
might be considered a series of still-life studies;
yet the uncanny aspect of their composition
and its a-scalar, a-perspectival nature
creates a curious paradox. Neither directly
representational nor entirely atmospheric,
the nature of the composition incites a search
for a coherent conceptual ordering system
through the application of which we might
gain a deeper understanding of the complex
semiotics on show.

Everything tends to make us believe that there exists a
certain point of the mind at which life and death, the real
and the imagined, past and future, the communicable and
the incommunicable, high and low, cease to be perceived as
contradictions.
— André Breton, *The Second Manifesto of Surrealism,*
1929[1]

Riverrun, past heavenly horned Saint 'Eustachio with his
dog teeth, from the swerve of the dark forest of Signs
to the Palace of the Brine and bend of Bay, brings us by
Communicating Vessels back to our Interior Castle …
— Neil Spiller, "Halcyon Daze, Astonishing Panoramas,"
2024[2]

Born of the turbulent confluence of intuition, imagination, and
memory, creativity is a curious and often confounding thing.
Contingent on an uncanny conjunction—the serendipitous
syzygy of figments and fragments carried on the capricious
currents of chance—the creative impulse is often induced by
a state of visual confusion or cognitive dissonance. Classically
conceptualized as the fickle flirtations of the mischievous
Muse,[3] these unexpected epiphanies have long been intimately
linked to the esoteric orders of experiential embodiment and an
enaction of divine disclosure.

Irrespective of their exact origin, these inspirational
inducements must be rendered knowable and communicable,
transformed from tacit knowledge into some, more tangible, form.
Appearing neither instantaneously nor full formed ex nihilo, the
manifestation of these mediating objects often induces further
creative curiosity, forming a fecund feedback loop of action and
reflection that often challenges our original intent, allowing
unintended and unanticipated insights to emerge.

From the fantastic formulae of early alchemical treatises to the chimeric combines of Surreal art and literature, many of the artifacts created as a conduit to this latent realm of creative potential rely on an intentional ambiguity or multiplicity of meaning in order to cultivate confusion and harness it in pursuit of the creative cause. It is perhaps little wonder, then, that the fluidic free mixing of signs that we oh-so-reductively name "collage" holds a privileged position in the artistic imagination. Predicated on the recombination of found and foraged objects, elements, and artifacts, the collage constructs meaning through relational structuring rather than explicit illustration and direct representation.

Framed through this appropriative artistic epistemology, "The Sixth Somewhat Annual Meeting" exhibition at the A83 gallery in New York invited a group of internationally renowned artist-architects to select and re-work a set of archival prints from the gallery and printmaking studio's collection, in a form of multi-dimensional, multi-durational collage that sought to inspire a renewed creative curiosity among the participants.

Selecting a teasing triptych of purportedly purist paintings—*Egg*, *Angel*, and *Cornice* (1987) by the American artist architect Anthony Ames—British architectural maverick Neil Spiller (referred to hereafter only by his nom de guerre "the Professor") engaged in a doubled re-reading. His *Pluck's Gutter Mannequin Shop* (2024) offers a reconsideration of Ames's original work, constructed through the invention of an alchemically augmented praxis in which ambiguity became an unconventional ally in the quest for understanding.

Drawing on (pun intended) Ames's own interpretive works, which examine the complex and often contradictory machinic metaphors and purist symbolism of Modernist art and architecture,[4] the Professor's radical rearticulations explore our ongoing disciplinary obsession with the machinic allegory, while introducing a forward-facing thematic integer, the complex bio-technical wetware(s) of an impending, Post-Singularity "Synthetic Age"[5] of nano-machines and cyber-spatial hybridities.

Neil Spiller,
Venus enters the Mannequin Shop, "Halcyon Daze, Astonishing Panoramas" series, 2024

left: Intrinsically polymorphous, Venus is seen altering her aspect from her earlier atavistic manifestation as Aphrodite, and now dons the tripartite guise of Hecate, the ancient Greek goddess of transience and change, crossroads and witchcraft. As her form shifts, so too does the shop, as Modernist compositions give way to the metaphysical influences of the Italian artist Giorgio de Chirico. Simultaneously a set of measures emerges, charting this complex cognitive choreography, in a 'pataphysical play on the tension between implicit and explicit, empiric and artistic.

Neil Spiller,
Interior of the Mannequin Shop, "Halcyon Daze, Astonishing Panoramas" series, 2024

opposite: Adopting the typological trope of the Wunderkammer, the Mannequin Shop itself is an encyclopedic collection of formative figures and fragments. Established not only to allow Spiller to reflect on his many fascinations, it acts as an assemblage, a choreographed concatenation in which the proximities and positions of the various objects on display serve to synthesize meaning and aid the assimilation of new understandings.

Following in the footsteps of avant-garde novelists such as James Joyce,[6] Alfred Jarry,[7] and Angela Carter,[8] the Professor's tall tale belongs to the grand literary tradition in which the narrator recounts an uncanny encounter and the ensuing journey of experiential (self-)discovery that this unexpected event precipitates. Propelled by the provocative Prophet of Desire, our sardonic steersman Sharron (a homonymic double reference to the ancient Greek mythological figure Charon the ferryman who transported the souls of the dead to the afterlife, and Sharron, the Professor's former executive assistant—who was in turn responsible for keeping the Professor on course as he navigated the murky waters of academic management), we follow the Professor's progress as he is drawn on a dreamlike dérive[9] passing through a second-order psycho(geo)graphy of connotative constructs and artistic appropriations superimposed upon the slow sweeps and swerves of the Stour—a river that flows through the county of Kent in England, upon the banks of which the Professor, scab kneed and ruddy cheeked, played as a young boy.

Wending our way along the river, we pass through a numinous network of disconcertingly familiar signs and signifiers, from soaring spires, striped beach huts, and angular outlines of 1970s postmodern municipality, to marbled saints arched in ecstasy and Large Glass[10] windows, a maverick's memory palace of architectural archetypes and artistic tropes raided from a thousand varied sources.

At certain key (con)junctions, Venus (the other half of the desirous duo of diametrically opposed Jungian avatars that act as our aquatic guides) opposes Sharron's baser urge toward a permanent, perpetual motion, directing our disembarkation from Sharron's craft and inviting a more intimate encounter with some specific space or scene. Rendered mutable by these scenographic shifts in pace and perspective, the informative framework of once-recognizable referents is transformed, revealing new meaning as the moment of (un)certainty passes and the kaleidoscope of components coalesces. From Dalí-esque legs burdened with bread, to lasciviously laid-out temples of repose, and columns cast in the likeness of a certain putrefying portrait, each of these primordial, 'pataphysical prompts is but one of a set of samples,[11] a series of irreducible ideas and conceptual constants that form the intellectual *prima materia* of the "Communicating Vessels" project. Through the manipulation of these strange shamanic totems, the Professor performs his heuristic scryings and dialectic divinations, attempting to determine an architectonic future through a continual rereading of our disciplinary past.

All Aboard the Chemical Epiphany

Emerging abruptly, liberated by the lubrication action of the Professor's Potion of Panacea, in the heady heat of the summer of '24, the unanticipated outpouring of many thousands of words of prose and dozens of drawings would later crystallize into the "Halcyon Daze, Astonishing Panoramas" series (2024), a 'pataphysical prequel (though it might more accurately be considered an obliquel—an intellectually adjacent alternative telling) to the Professor's ongoing magnum opus, the "Communicating Vessels" project (1998–). Yet while "Communicating Vessels" explores architecture's relationship to various emergent technologies, from cyber-spatial congruences to nano-machinic marvels, "Halcyon Daze" is an altogether more human affair. Occupying the dialectic tensions between time and place, love and lust, it is a Rebis thing, a dream(ing) theater of facts, fictions, and fantasies.

Disgusting Dialectic Demonstrations

But we are getting ahead of ourselves, no doubt seduced by the sumptuous stimuli of the Professor's provocatively prophetic path. Although we have already alluded to the importance of rereading and reinterpreting earlier work as an essential aspect of any critically creative enterprise, before we can proceed further on this voyeuristic voyage, we must first establish the practices and process that allow this (re)new(ed) knowledge to manifest. Of the many mediatory methods at our collective creative disposal, drawing is perhaps the most frequently associated with the architect's praxis.

Established throughout the creative disciplines as a core communicative practice, drawing is a form of informational exchange based on visual, often pictorial, representation. Architecture extends this broader communicative capacity, conceptualizing the drawing as a mediating object—a synthetic condition in which projective imagining meets observational recording, allowing the reflective and reflexive testing of intuition against a variety of internal and external factors and explicit and implicit constraints.

From the development of details to evocative explorations of atmospheric experience, irrespective of the medium and manner of its execution, while drawing is a process, an experiential enaction of understanding, the drawing itself is often viewed as a didactic demonstration of architectonic intent. As uncertainty is erased in favor of reductive resolution, this troubling tendency toward descriptive denotation brings with it a forfeiture of imaginative, inspirational ambiguity.

Of Dream(s) and Actuality

In his seminal re-telling *Polyphilo, or The Dark Forest Revisited* (1992),[12] noted architectural theorist and historian Alberto Pérez-Gómez attempts to challenge the emergence of illustrative instrumentality as a dominant form of architectural thought, through a reconsideration of the enigmatic and evasive Renaissance treatise the *Hypnerotomachia Poliphili* (1499).[13]

Transporting us on a transcendent flight of technospheric fantasy, Pérez-Gómez attempts to navigate and negotiate the ontological complexities of the architectural experience. Drawing connections to the esoteric art of alchemy, a proto-scientific philosophy preoccupied with the transmutation of mundane matter(s), he posits that architectural meaning is predicated on a cycle of fragmentation and union, a paradoxical palingenesis of prior knowledge that implicates both a temporal component and the body as the pre-reflective ground of experience.[14] Emerging from this dialectical dance of irreconcilable opposites, architecture, he eventually concludes, is a product of (un)fulfilled desire mediated by the erotic impulse.[15]

Embracing the dynamic dualism of this hermetic ontology, the Professor augments his representational practices, allegorically reconceptualizing the drawing as an alchemic alembic, the twin-chambered vessel of ritual recombination and reconstitution.

At once singular and serial, combining techniques of collage and a parallel practice of palincestuously reprojecting earlier iterations, or whole drawings, back onto the picture plane. As the drawing becomes saturated with these concurrent compositions, it takes on the dreamlike aspect of hypnagogia. Rendered soluble by the ambiguity of their new-found oneiric aspect, these image objects are transformed from sign-signifiers into allegorical or metaphorical exchange values. As the unexpected and serendipitous emerge from this phantasmagorical profundity of figments and fragments, the transformative capacities of collage are enhanced and intensified by the introduction of the ambiguous surface and the uncertain durational dynamic, opening the possibility for multiple readings and innumerable interpretations as components shift and new proximities and positions emerge.

Throughout this mysterious miasma, the Professor's plump black lines[16] swerve, inscribing and incising the vectors of unfolding, weaving a tangled tapestry of pluralistic presents, future fragments, and historic hauntings.

Neil Spiller,
*Meat Curtains, Pluck's Gutter
Mannequin Shop,* "Halcyon Daze,
Astonishing Panoramas" series,
2024

opposite: Named after the adolescent slang for pronounced labia majora, the synthetic spatial screen that divides the shop serves as more than just humorous metaphor. It instead betrays a much more evocative conception of the drawing as a gestatory environment for the inception and conception of ideas.

Neil Spiller,
*Half-finished Mannequin, Pluck's
Gutter Mannequin Shop,* "Halcyon
Daze,
Astonishing Panoramas" series,
2024

left: As the dreamlike drawings unfold, we are often left wondering whether we have moved or whether the scene has shifted. Formed from fragments of the shop's façade, Venus's transmogrification, and other less identifiable matter(s), this mannequin emerges (half) formed and unfinished, reminding us of the cycle of putrefaction and rebirth while raising complex questions of completion and wholeness that await further (de) constructive attention.

Neil Spiller,
Handler of Gravity, Pluck's Gutter Mannequin Shop, "Halcyon Daze, Astonishing Panoramas" series, "The Sixth Somewhat Annual Meeting" exhibition, A83 gallery, New York, 2025

opposite: The referents we encounter within Spiller's 'Pataphysically projected dreamscapes are not just architectural and literary. They are frequently inspired by various contemporary and classical works of art, science, and philosophy—here, Newton's discovery of the titular universal force meets the body in a carefully choreographed encounter.

Neil Spiller,
Sore, Leaky Blobs, Pluck's Gutter Mannequin Shop, "Halcyon Daze, Astonishing Panoramas" series, 2024

above: Transposed into an alternative format, the third mannequin lies in a state of repose, perhaps a reference to Spiller's cyber-spatial temple? Where other mannequins appear artificial, the third construct we encounter has a far more biological form.

Perpetual (E)motion

Applying his esoteric artistry to Ames's already uncannily aperspectival vistas, the Professor works through an iterative and invasive process of edits and interventions, layering and splicing drawn figments and harvested fragments into the original paintings. Paradoxically pluralized by this dense digital stratum of simultaneous, superpositioned surfaces, the curiously compressed picture planes of Ames's original works become increasingly unstable, as the concurrent compositions clash and collide, competing for the viewer's attention.

Oscillating with barely contained erotic potential, the Professor's serial(ized) visions and vistas of the *Pluck's Gutter Mannequin Shop* reveal a charnel house of desirous devices and trashed flesh cages, a cyberspatiality-saturated biotechnical birthing ground, that heralds a new machinic order. Yet while the threateningly fetishistic forms of these curious constructs might evoke a disquieting sense of estrangement, so too do they provoke a desirous urge for a deeper, more carnal form of knowing.

Examined more intimately, these enigmatic enfoldings reveal a complex catalogue of referents, the irreconcilable tensions between man and nature, machine and metaphysics, logic and lust, our disciplinary DNA—the *prima materia* of architecture's own magnum opus—locked in a continuous cycle of (re) generative palingenesis. Held in the arms of Venus, these deeper meanings eagerly anticipate discovery, like lovers impatiently awaiting the caress of those that would care to know them. ∆

Notes
1. André Breton, *Manifestoes of Surrealism* [1962], tr. Richard Seaver and Helen Lane, University of Michigan Press (Ann Arbor), 2010, p. 123.
2. Neil Spiller, "Halcyon Daze, Astonishing Panoramas," unpublished text, 2024, p. 1.
3. Karl Kerényi, *The Gods of the Greeks*, Thames & Hudson (London), 1951, p. 100.
4. See Anthony Ames, *Fifty Paintings: Anthony Ames Architect*, ORO Editions (San Francisco), 2021.
5. See K. Eric Dexter, *Engines of Creation: The Coming Era of Nanotechnology*, Anchor Books (New York), 1986.
6. See James Joyce, *Finnegans Wake* [1939], Read Books (London), 2010.
7. See Alfred Jarry, *Exploits and Opinions of Dr. Faustroll, Pataphysician*, tr. Simon Watson Taylor, Exact Change (Cambridge, MA), 1996.
8. See Angela Carter, *The Infernal Desire Machines of Doctor Hoffman*, Rupert Hart Davis (London), 1972.
9. See Guy Debord, "Theory of the Dérive" [1958], tr. Kenneth Knabb, in *Situationist International Anthology*, Bureau of Public Secrets (Berkeley, CA), rev. edn. 2006, pp. 62–6.
10. See Calvin Tomkins, *Duchamp: A Biography*, Henry Holt & Company (New York), 1996, p. 48.
11. Carter, *The Infernal Desire Machines of Doctor Hoffman*, p. 110.
12. Alberto Pérez-Gómez, *Polyphilo, or The Dark Forest Revisited: An Erotic Epiphany of Architecture* [1992], MIT Press (Cambridge, MA), 1994.
13. See Francesco Colonna, *Hypnerotomachia Poliphili* [1499], Thames & Hudson (London), 2005.
14. See Maurice Merleau-Ponty, *Phenomenology of Perception*, tr. Donald Landes, Routledge (London), 2012, pp. 100–101.
15. Pérez-Gómez, *Polyphilo*, p. xvii.
16. See Neil Spiller, *Burning Whiteness, Plump Black Lines: The Projects of Spiller Farmer Architects*, Spiller Farmer Publications (London), 1990.

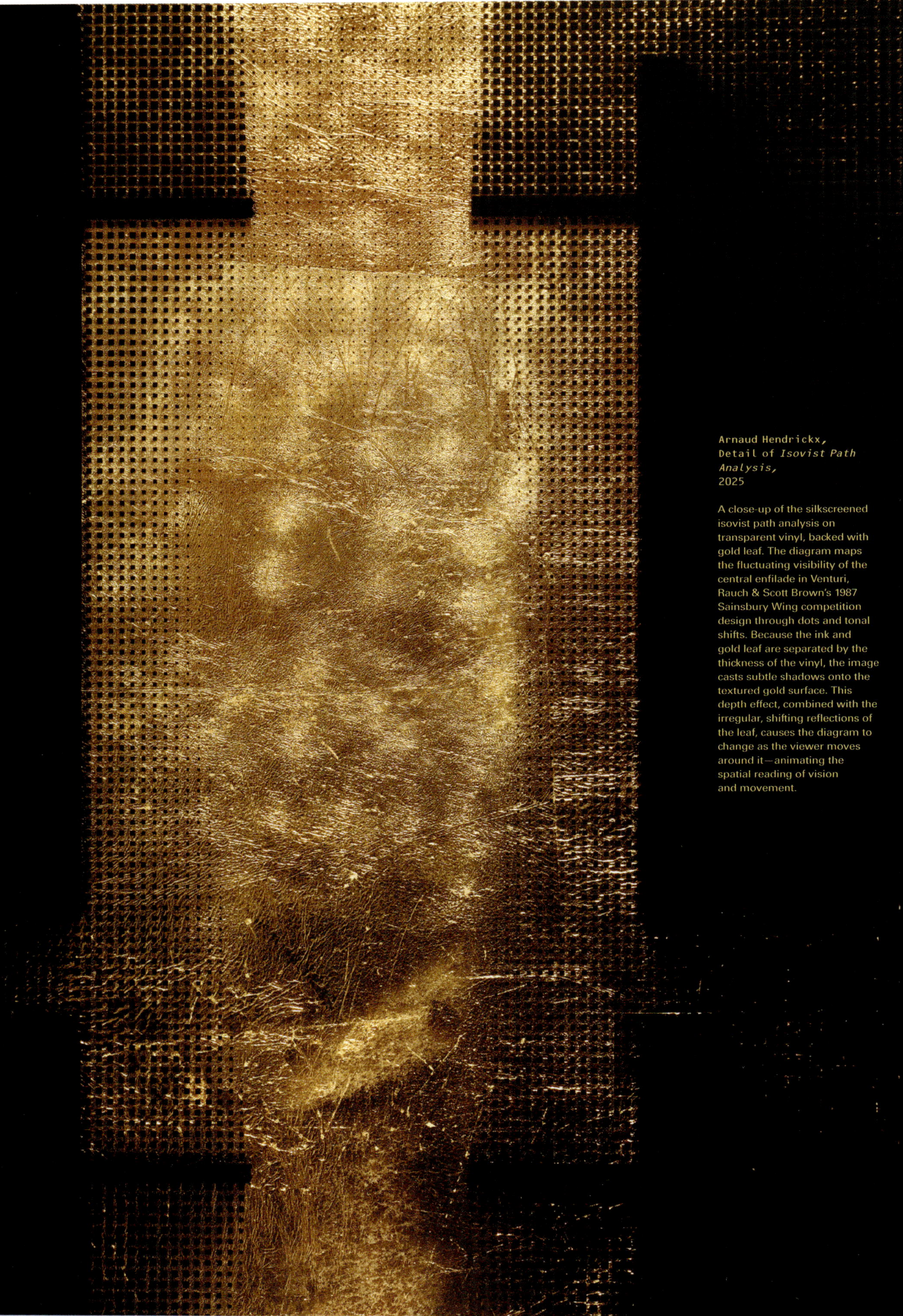

Arnaud Hendrickx,
Detail of *Isovist Path Analysis,*
2025

A close-up of the silkscreened isovist path analysis on transparent vinyl, backed with gold leaf. The diagram maps the fluctuating visibility of the central enfilade in Venturi, Rauch & Scott Brown's 1987 Sainsbury Wing competition design through dots and tonal shifts. Because the ink and gold leaf are separated by the thickness of the vinyl, the image casts subtle shadows onto the textured gold surface. This depth effect, combined with the irregular, shifting reflections of the leaf, causes the diagram to change as the viewer moves around it—animating the spatial reading of vision and movement.

Bart Verschaffel

Revisiting Venturi, Rauch & Scott Brown's Sainsbury Wing of the National Gallery, London

Like Thom Mayne and Morphosis' 6th Street Residence, the drawings of Venturi, Rauch & Scott Brown's Sainsbury Wing inspired more than one drawer or printmaker in the group. Belgian architect Arnaud Hendrickx explored the enfilade arrangements of the Wing's galleries, deriving from them a sculptural piece and representing this form in a series of gold-colored prints. Hendrickx's preoccupations align with his other research on the overlapping of art and architecture and its fecund interstices. **Bart Verschaffel**, a philosopher, and Emeritus Professor at Ghent University, extrapolates Hendrickx's interests further.

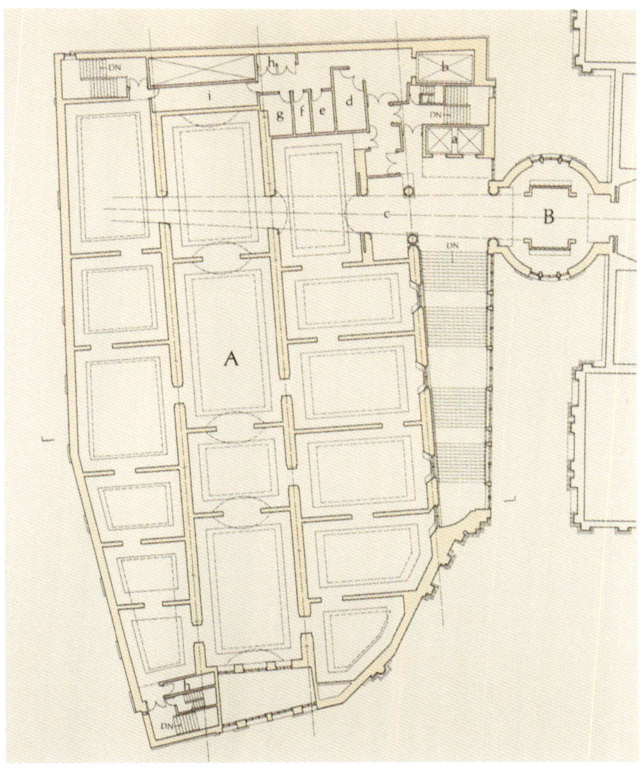

Venturi, Rauch & Scott Brown,
Competition design for the
Sainsbury Wing extension to the
National Gallery,
London,
1987

This gallery-level floor plan was produced as part of the competition entry. The drawing was screenprinted that same year by John Nichols Printmakers & Publishers at the site now occupied by A83 in New York. Several test prints remain in A83's archive and later served as the basis for Arnaud Hendrickx's reconstructed drawing and spatial analysis.

The architect Arnaud Hendrickx, previously associate of the architectural studio RAUW, and currently professor at the Faculty of Architecture, KU Leuven—Campus Sint-Lucas in Brussels, now works mainly in the area between art and architecture. Invited by the New York-based printmaking studio and gallery A83 to select an architectural drawing from their archive and create a work in response to it for the "The Sixth Somewhat Annual Meeting" exhibition in 2025, he chose a ground plan of the competition-winning proposal by Venturi, Rauch & Scott Brown for the expansion of the Sainsbury Wing of the National Gallery in London's Trafalgar Square, which was realized in 1991. It was one of the most important and most discussed architectural projects of the time and an icon of Postmodernism. Both the then traditionalist movement in British architecture and Late Modernists rejected the "complexity" of the design with which Venturi, Rauch & Scott Brown affirmed and brilliantly resolved the tensions and contradictions regarding the location, materials, construction, program, and style of the project. The façade design in particular—which first aligns with the historic building, adopts its scale, rhythm, and stylistic elements, and then gradually turns into a glass side wall—was highly controversial. The competition drawing chosen by Hendrickx, however, shows not a view or elevation of the disputed façade but a ground plan.

On the interior, Venturi, Rauch & Scott Brown's design for the Sainsbury Wing consists mainly of an entrance hall, with public functions and spaces for temporary exhibitions slid underneath, a monumental staircase added on the east side of the existing building, and an upper floor with added gallery spaces. The staircase gradually widens upward, correcting the slightly oblique position of the Sainsbury Wing relative to the main museum building. The staircase leads to the *piano nobile* containing the permanent collection. The main intervention in the exhibition areas themselves is to use arches to structure the sightlines and give rhythm to the walk-through.

Arnaud Hendrickx,
Reconstructed Perspective View of the Central Enfilade in Venturi, Rauch & Scott Brown's 1987 Sainsbury Wing Competition Design,
2025

Based on archival documents from the 1987 competition, a three-dimensional reconstruction of the Sainsbury Wing was developed. This image presents a rendering of the gallery spaces, capturing the enfilade's spatial depth through its sequence of gilded frames and paintings (extracted from a photograph by Matt Wargo). The vantage point closely aligns with that of *The Enderman of the Sainsbury Wing* (2025), while the golden accents echo the metonymic link between representation and subject explored in *Isovist Path Analysis* (2025).

By combining the visibility analysis of many viewpoints of the Gallery into one drawing, Hendrickx's *Isovist Path Analysis* (2025) transforms a *document* into a *monument*

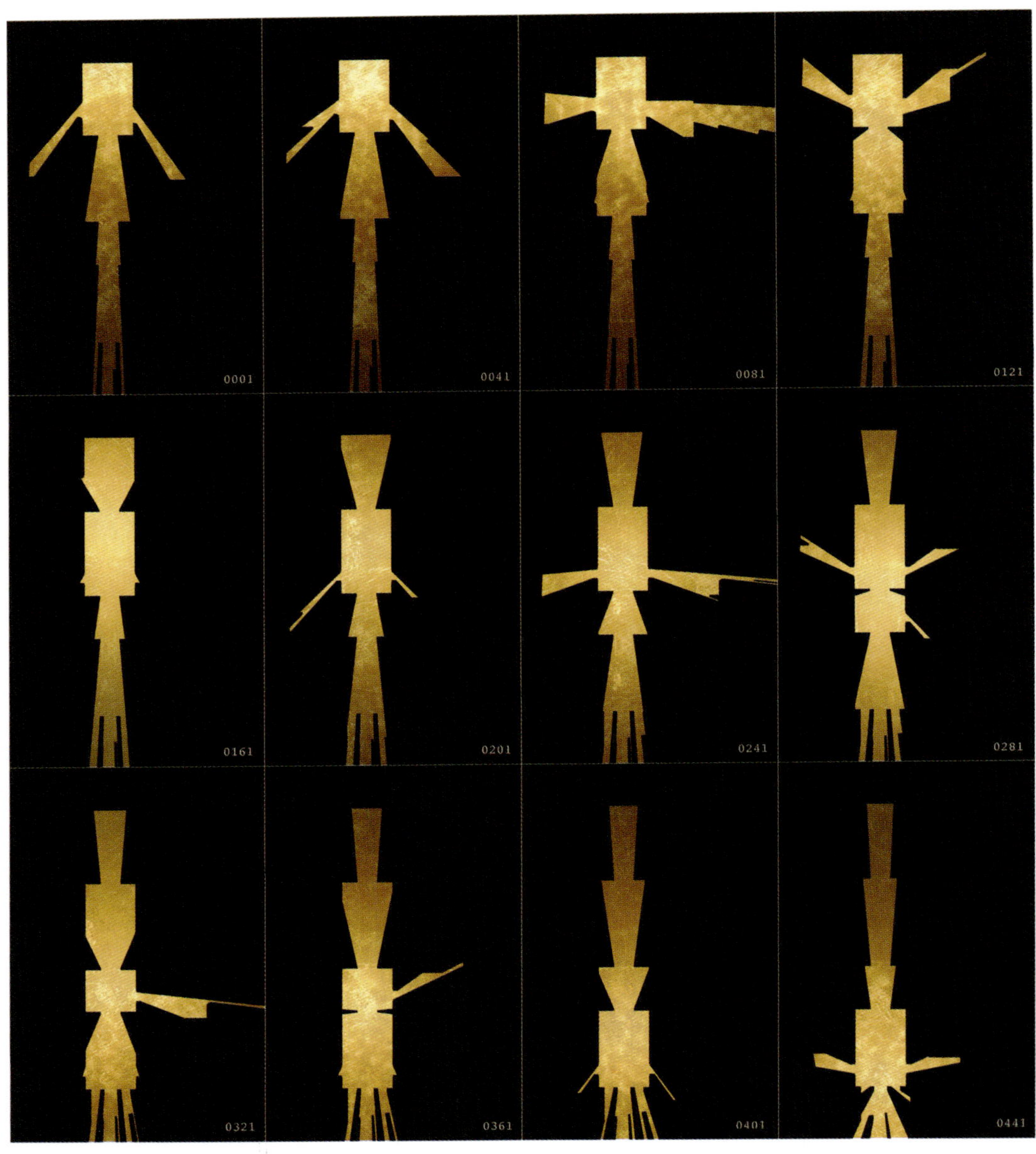

Arnaud Hendrickx,
Visibility Simulation Frames of the Central Enfilade in Venturi, Rauch & Scott Brown's 1987 Sainsbury Wing Competition Design,
2025

A sequence of stills from a dynamic visibility simulation, in which a moving light source scans a 3D reconstruction of Venturi, Rauch & Scott Brown's design. Each frame captures a moment of spatial exposure, rendered as irregular black forms set against a gold-leaf background. These momentary fields of vision articulate the fluctuating reach of sight through the enfilade.

Venturi, Rauch & Scott Brown's drawing is not a design sketch, perspective, or technical drawing, but a presentation drawing of the floor plan—informative, and drawn in the idiom of the classical architectural tradition. The experience of space and architecture is always very complex, at once visual, synesthetic, and very physical; difficult to capture in words. What happens when architectural drawings are detached from the context of a building process, and end up in an artistic context, as in the projects of a studio like A83, or in an artwork by Hendrickx? What do they convey? Evidently, the aesthetic aspect is separated from the many other functions of the architectural drawing and particularly emphasized. But the appropriation and context shift do more than that.

Important architectural projects by renowned architects are nowadays sufficiently documented and archived anyway. It is different with volatile architectural thinking and the architectural imagination. This is what the exercise of editing and responding to drawings, as within the A83 exhibition project, captures. By combining the visibility analysis of many viewpoints of the Gallery into one drawing, Hendrickx's *Isovist Path Analysis* (2025) transforms a *document* into a *monument*. It thus memorizes architectural thinking through a detour, preserving architectural work in entirely different ways to that of an architectural archive. That is, not as available information, but as an encrypted sign, like a Baroque emblem depicts and preserves an idea. Hendrickx's artistic monumentalization here combines two operations: the first, metaphorical, is the transformation of a ground plan or sketch into a diagram; the second, metonymical, is the effective or material linking of the represented subject or referent to the representation or the drawing itself by a gold coating.

Arnaud Hendrickx,
Accumulated Visibility Heatmap (Isovist Composite) of the Central Enfilade in Venturi, Rauch & Scott Brown's 1987 Sainsbury Wing Competition Design,
2025

A composite rendering combining hundreds of simulation frames into a single black-and-white heatmap. The image translates visibility into a dense grid of square pixels that grow or shrink depending on how many positions each point is visible from. This cumulative field models the overall spatial accessibility from the Sainsbury Wing gallery's central axis.

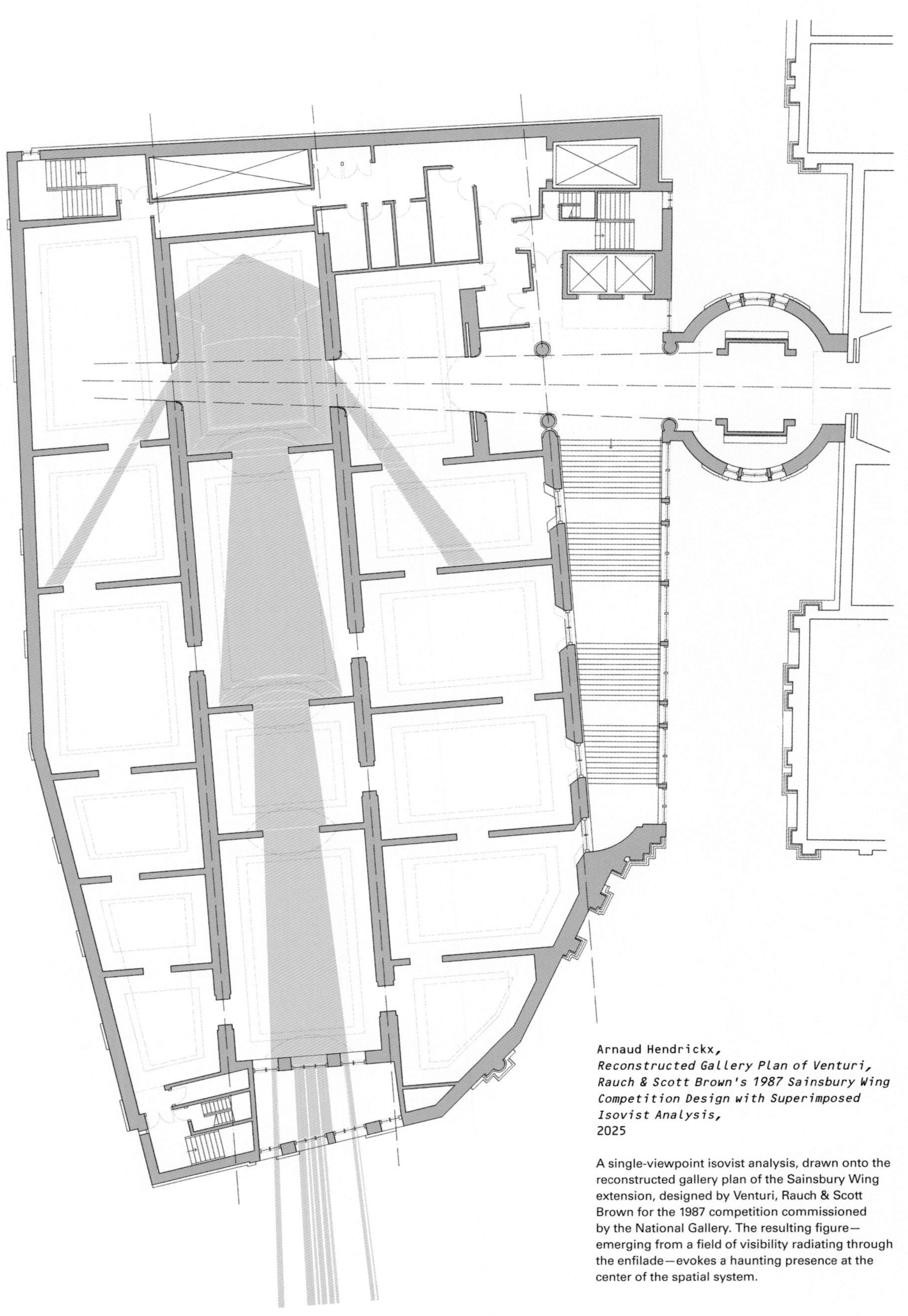

Arnaud Hendrickx,
*Reconstructed Gallery Plan of Venturi,
Rauch & Scott Brown's 1987 Sainsbury Wing
Competition Design with Superimposed
Isovist Analysis,*
2025

A single-viewpoint isovist analysis, drawn onto the reconstructed gallery plan of the Sainsbury Wing extension, designed by Venturi, Rauch & Scott Brown for the 1987 competition commissioned by the National Gallery. The resulting figure—emerging from a field of visibility radiating through the enfilade—evokes a haunting presence at the center of the spatial system.

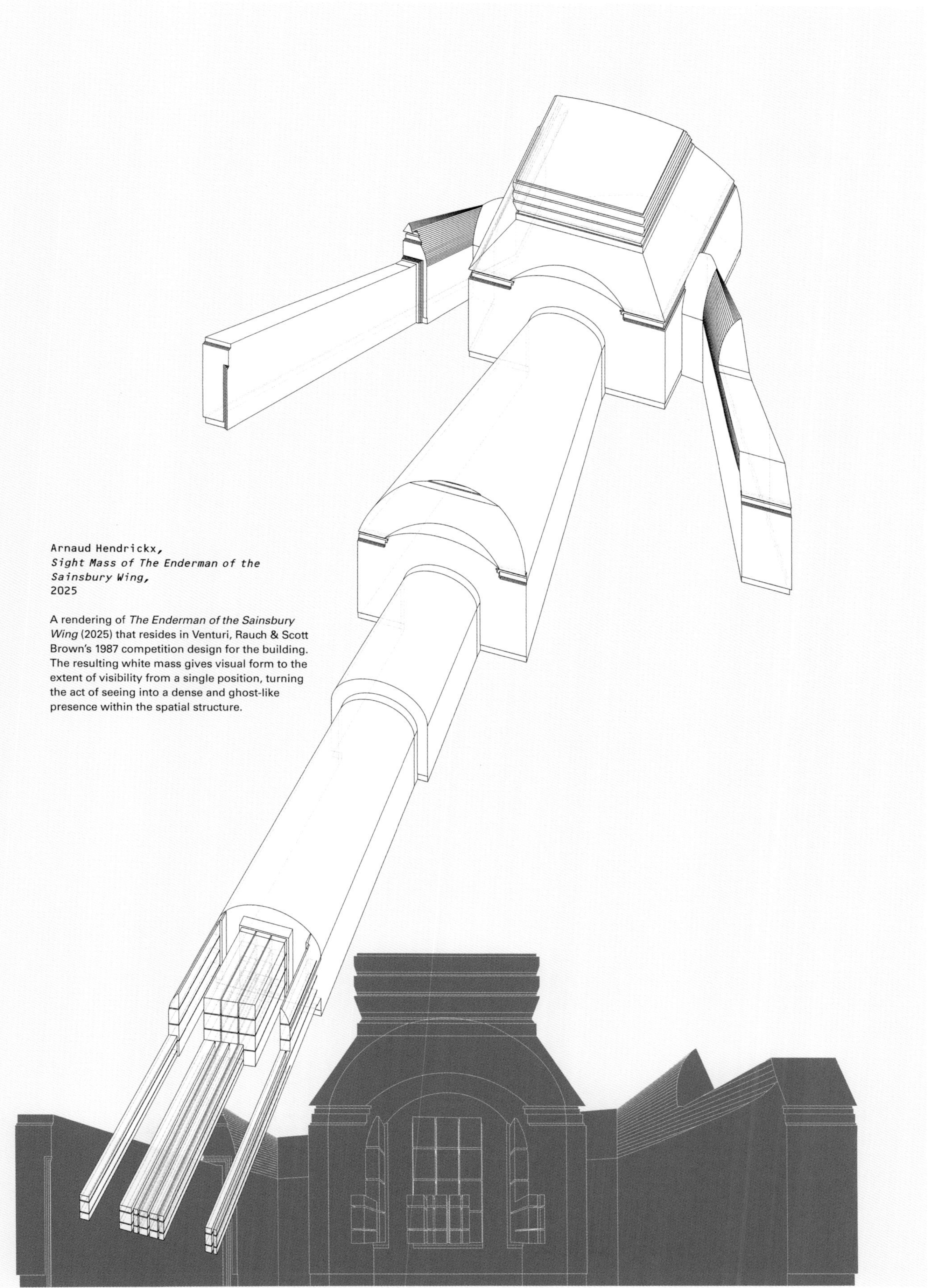

Arnaud Hendrickx,
Sight Mass of The Enderman of the Sainsbury Wing,
2025

A rendering of *The Enderman of the Sainsbury Wing* (2025) that resides in Venturi, Rauch & Scott Brown's 1987 competition design for the building. The resulting white mass gives visual form to the extent of visibility from a single position, turning the act of seeing into a dense and ghost-like presence within the spatial structure.

Transforming, Transposing

Hendrickx retains from the floor plan of the Sainsbury Wing only the central space: the Grande Galerie, the imposing heart of all classical museums. The "great gallery" combines the rhetoric of overview and the dictative, organizing gaze with that of ordered multiplicity and infinity. It elevates the gaze, and lessens the body—with examples including the Grande Galerie of the Louvre, as depicted by the French painter Hubert Robert in 1796, and the Modernist variant in Frank Lloyd Wright's Guggenheim Museum in New York of 1959. Unlike most such galleries, the one in the renovated Sainsbury Wing is divided by arches to form an enfilade of four rooms. The axial structure, continuity, and spatial depth effects thereby become much more complex due to the partition, and are comparable to the visuality of the early architectural perspective fantasies in Giovanni Battista Piranesi's *Prima Parte di Architetture e Prospettive* of 1743. The promenade thus becomes much more visually surprising and rich: the arches constantly hide and reveal the sidewalls with the paintings and the visitors who are viewing them. The constant discovery of new works, the constant appearance and disappearance of the other visitors, dynamize the walk and the experience of space.

Hendrickx's new drawing depicts and isolates this complex visuality. It shows not *what* can be seen; it is not about the paintings, but about *how* one can look. The drawing represents an isovist path analysis that notes with dots and tint differences the fluctuating "visibility" during a linear walk-through of the gallery, depending on the continuously changing viewpoints. Venturi, Rauch & Scott Brown's drawing is thus transformed into a diagram, and the shape of the diagram as such—using the philosopher Charles Peirce's semiotic vocabulary—produces a "quasi-iconic" result, and a new drawing. Hendrickx's work is a print with, on the left, the isovist path diagram of the Gallery of the Sainsbury Wing, and on the right, an enlargement of the diagram of the southern end. The drawing isolates the Gallery from the original project, and at once subtly corrects the ground plan. In Venturi, Rauch & Scott Brown's drawing, the new side façade of the Sainsbury Wing, with the staircase broadening upwards, forms the vertical, in parallel with the side façade of the National Gallery. As a result, the Gallery is slightly angled. This is straightened out—literally—in Hendrickx's drawing. The end result is an independent drawing that blends the specifics of an architectural plan into the generality of a quasi-abstract form.

Arnaud Hendrickx,
Isovist Path Analysis and
*The Enderman of the Sainsbury
Wing,* A83 gallery,
New York,
2025

Photograph of the diptych as exhibited in the group exhibition "The Sixth Somewhat Annual Meeting." The two works—conceived as spatial companions—juxtapose cumulative and singular isovist analyses, drawing attention to the shifting thresholds of visibility, movement, and material presence.

Transmitting Brilliance

The second decisive choice of Hendrickx's appropriation concerns the execution of the print. This is a silkscreen printed with black paint on a transparent bearer, the back of which is then beset with gold paint. In this way a gold shimmer is blended into the visual appearance of the print, thus creating a *pars pro toto* impression of the visuality in the museum gallery itself. After all, classical museum architecture, including the National Gallery, likes to use gold to highlight architectural elements such as ceilings and domes, architectural details such as capitals, doors, and ornaments, and so on. Glitter conspicuously evokes wealth and exuberance, and many paintings have impressive gilded frames. More than a conventional symbol, however, the radiance is the first, most primitive place where the image emerges: the image—see the icon, see the golden background in Byzantine and early Italian painting—is carried by the radiance, so that it manifests itself by itself. The gold leaf on Hendrickx's print literally connects, and thus establishes contact, with the seeing that the isovist diagram schematically represents. His work is thus not just a transformation, but a carry-over of a seemingly secondary element of the museum architectural experience. Just as the drawing isolates the visuality in the Sainsbury Wing gallery, transforms it into an abstract form, and generalizes it, the insertion of the gold layer isolates an essential ingredient of the (classical) museum experience, but detaches it from its specific references, evokes new associations, and thus creates a new, independent work.

The Enderman

Besides the print, which appropriates and transforms Venturi, Rauch & Scott Brown's drawing but remains within the same medium, the exhibition project included an object with sculptural and thus almost monumental allure: *The Enderman of the Sainsbury Wing*, a replica of the volume of the interior of the enfilade as seen in central perspective from the north side, where the visitor enters the gallery. The isovist diagram is the result of a plurality of points of view; *The Enderman*, a 3D-printed model, materializes only one dominant point of view. As the gaze penetrates the successive arcades and halls, the "size" of the gaze space becomes narrower and longer. This perspectival gaze, that embodies the basic principle of the spatiality of the Sainsbury Wing, and of classical architecture in general, was thus literally transformed into an object, viewed from the outside, objectified. It is not a scale model of an architectural space, but a solidification of a perceived space—just as the archaeologists at Pompeii make visible the cavities left by vanished bodies, or "print" them by filling them with plaster. ◪

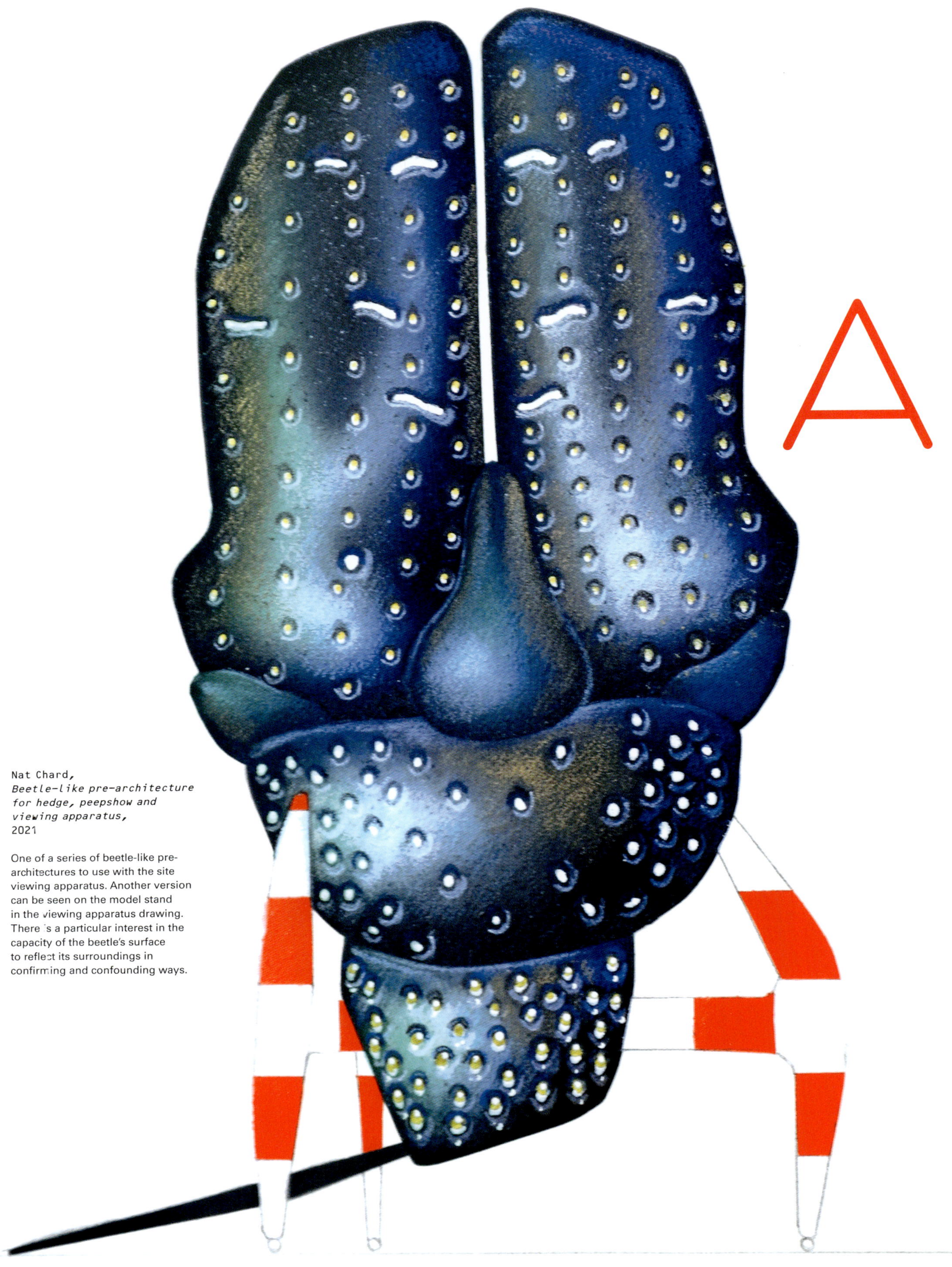

Nat Chard,
*Beetle-like pre-architecture
for hedge, peepshow and
viewing apparatus,*
2021

One of a series of beetle-like pre-architectures to use with the site viewing apparatus. Another version can be seen on the model stand in the viewing apparatus drawing. There is a particular interest in the capacity of the beetle's surface to reflect its surroundings in confirming and confounding ways.

Alex Pillen

Floating World

NAT CHARD'S OPTICAL-MATERIAL EXPERIMENTS

The works of London architect Nat Chard, Bartlett professor at University College London (UCL), have always had a highly finished yet enigmatic presence. Chard is interested in various aspects of optics such as, stereography, parallax, picture planes, movement, and perception. **Alex Pillen** is an artist, anthropologist, and Associate Professor in the Department of Anthropology at UCL. Here she casts her eye on recent work and, in a dialogue with Chard, seeks to explain his graphic, architectural, and intellectual strivings.

Nat Chard can perhaps best be called an architect of a floating world. For this article he chose to be interviewed by an anthropologist. There was no need for questions. What followed was a long conversation about flying paint, dots, parallax, paradoxical shadows, clouds, non-Newtonian fluids, blood, the human body, floating arcs, peep shows, and dioramas. All of these matter to conceptualize Chard's contribution to the "Sixth Somewhat Annual Meeting" exhibition held at the A83 gallery in New York during February and March 2025. Not one of these elements can be left out of this story that unfolds gradually, from process to process, over 35 years of architectural experiment.

For the Russian literary critic and philosopher Mikhail Bakhtin, each word we utter is a "shared territory" of meaning.[1] Language is understood in spatial terms, as a space shared by a speaker and their listener. In the same vein, an object engenders a shared dwelling for artist and viewer. A Bakhtinian notion of that shared space leads us to envisage its actual shape. This is an architectural space that amounts to a physical imagination of a postmodern condition. Chard's process appears as a visual intervention in that space—a virtual space of post-structuralism, a place for continuous contextual interpretation, conceived as a ground for his experiments. His work pushes the space's contours, perhaps stretching them so far that the familiar metaphors pop. A shared territory of meaning, a post-structuralist space, appears poked from the inside. Its shape is changing through an experimental architecture, beyond the comfort of that shared territory of contextual interpretation. Chard does this through a suspension of context. He is led by a unique process, a Chardean visual intervention that dislodges the edifice of post-structuralism built upon a foundation of contextual support. In his oeuvre, contextual clues become attenuated, sidelined, and spatial intuitions are called into question.

A Floating World

How does Chard create a suspension of context? Easier said than done, but essential to becoming an architect of a floating world. Referring to the paint from a previous work, he says, "You know it is a non-Newtonian fluid, just like blood." The non-Newtonian—his use of a material that does not follow Newton's laws of fluid dynamics—is given precedence over other topics. This is latex paint that changes viscosity when you apply force to it. His comment is about an earlier piece, an instrument of uncertainty that features a paint catapult. The image to retain here is of a flying splatter of viscous paint. Not paint obeying Newtonian laws of physics, when settled on a brush, palette, or canvas. It is flying, and almost seems to float when caught with high-speed flash photography. The context of gravity dissolves into the background in that brief moment of suspension.

Chard's experimental practice alerts us to ideas that are beyond the reasonable certainty of the

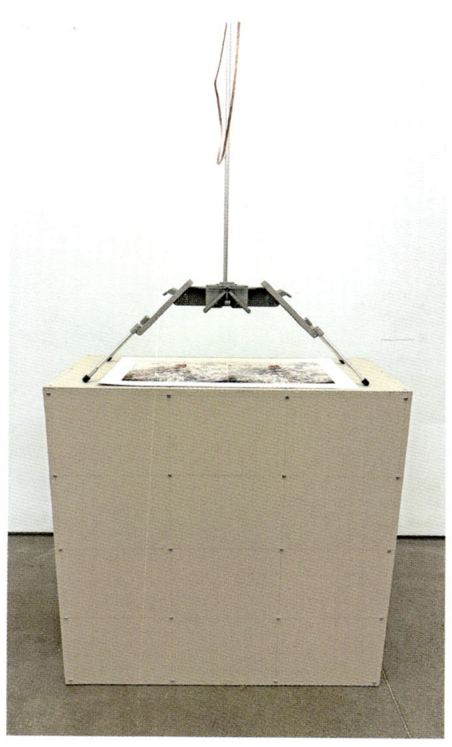

opposite: To tease out the potential of working with A83's printing expertise, this stereoscopic print twice uses the dots inherent in screenprinting's color separation process. The pictorial image represented through the dots operates in the conventional way to produce a three-dimensional image, while the parallax between the dots on the left- and right-eye images form their own independent 3D image (in this case a sloping surface). The latter will not be apparent here due to the scale of reproduction.

Nat Chard,
Hedge with floating shadow peepshow print and mirror stereoscope, "The Sixth Somewhat Annual Meeting" exhibition, A83 gallery, New York, 2025

left: The spatial images created by the pictorial and coloration separation dots are made apparent using a mirror stereoscope. The size of the print corresponds to the breadth of view of the stereoscope.

Nat Chard,
Site viewing apparatus,
2025

below: The floating shadow peepshow in the stereoscopic print is a fragment of a larger apparatus that plays with the capacity of shadows and reflections to relate an architectural model (and subsequently the resulting architecture) to its site, while at the same time separating it from it. The image incorporates a frame to hold the peepshow, a frame to hold architectural models, a malleable lightbox, and a synthetic hedge.

architectural program. We ought to learn from the uncertain, rather than from just the predictable. Such uncertainty is not easy to put into words. The image of that flying paint and the other instruments of uncertainty Chard built seem stronger than words. This is a form of "tacit knowledge." However, his architectural oeuvre does not neatly fit into the box of a "tacit dimension" articulated by the polymath Michael Polanyi.[2] Chard conceives of physical manifestations that are not about tacit values, prejudgments, or prediction. Instead, what he invokes is a tacit sense of the uncertain, the unfathomable, the unpredictable. The flying non-Newtonian splatter of paint is a figurative rendering of such a tacit condition. A condition that is almost never recognized or given shape in our tangible physical world. His attention to non-Newtonian behavior and the figuration of uncertainty is only one of the ways in which Nat experiments and unearths such tacit knowledge.

One of the field study instruments that work in conjunction with the viewing apparatus. The relationship between clouds and a place varies, from site-specific clouds such as the Levanter that sits above the Rock of Gibraltar (or the clouds attached to Mount Fuji) to clouds that have a character almost completely independent of their location. The bored cloud chamber explores possible resonances between clouds and their location.

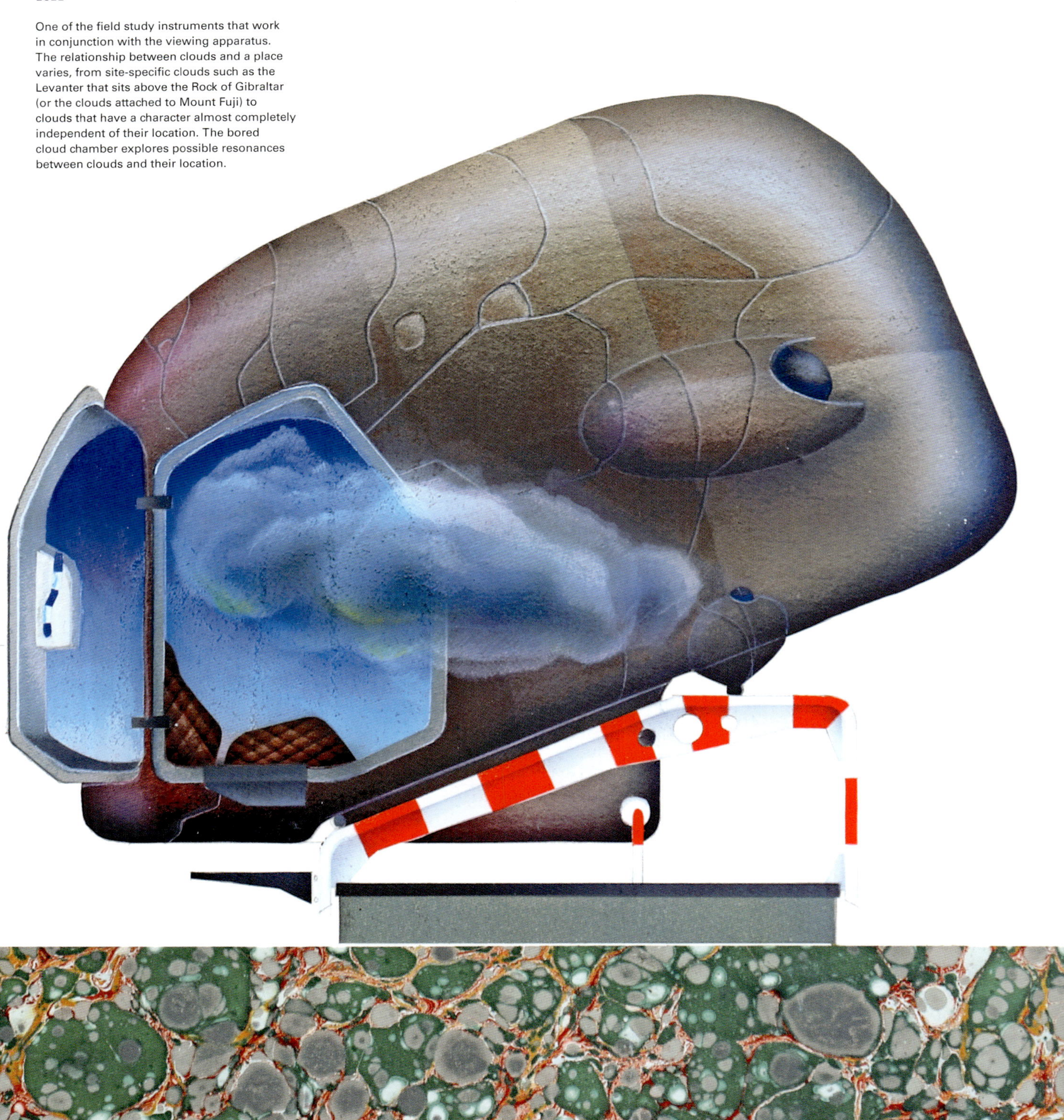

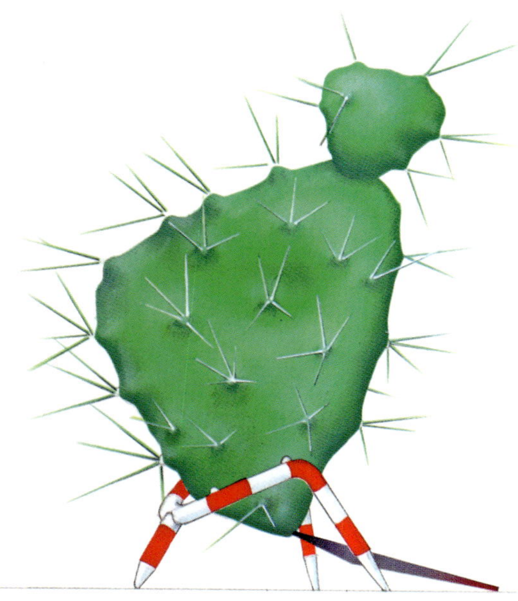

Early drawn studies look at
naturally occurring plants
and insects that can establish
tantalizing relationships with their
environments and translate them
into a pre-architectural entity to
use as a testing model on the site
viewing apparatus.

As an architect of a floating world, he also conceives of floating shadows, shadows untethered from the weight of an object, the physique of a light source. Such shadows are no longer the captives of things. Chard has paid attention to shadows since his early days working with dioramas and stereoscopic photography and was drawn toward paradoxical shadows. These are shadows that you perceive as floating—their origin is nowhere to be seen. The experience of a floating shadow points at an adventurous form of perception often challenged by a rather conservative consciousness about objects and their shadows. Here Chard drives a wedge between perception and that kind of consciousness. With two light sources and polarizing filters he catches the shadow in "mid-air," just like he did with that splatter of paint. He then introduces us to an atlas of floating shadows.

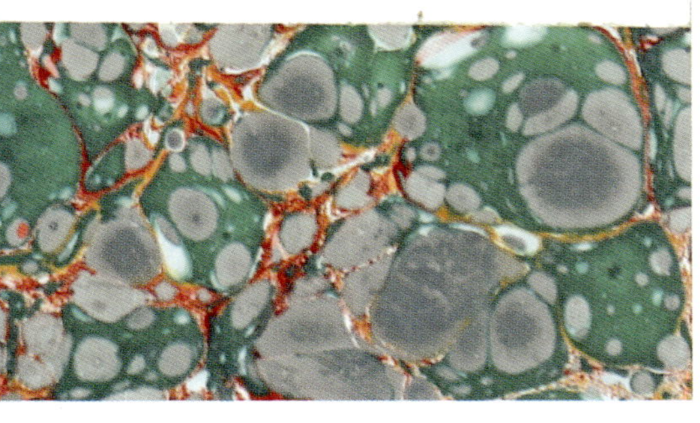

This is not only about the dichotomy of perception and consciousness. The notion of memory or the recollection of a moment is also central to Chard's oeuvre. As the flying paint hits an object, the splatter is a recollection of that meeting between paint and object. Chard wonders if shadows could be made in the same way, as a recollection in the absence of an object. He tweaks that triadic structure of perception, memory, and consciousness. The contextual markers of experience no longer fully support one another. This is a distinct technique or suspension of context that offers us glimpses of a floating world.

A New Departure, A83, New York

So what made the *Hedge with floating shadow peepshow and floating picture plane* work that Chard exhibited at A83 in New York different from all the above? Chard had worked with parallax before—the parallax for left- and right-eye views, or parallax created with two light sources. At A83 the method was different. Here he created a floating plane made out of a screenprint of dots. He used a double parallax technique as one plane of floating dots is inclined, tilted, while the other is parallel to the surface of the image. This process is similar to the one producing the floating shadow in the peepshow, but different in a fundamental way. The viewer looked at the image through a veil, an image wrapped into a floating plane of dots.

In cultural terms, Chard's dotted screenprint should not go unnoticed. The literature on this topic in anthropology is vast, and there is only room to mention a few elements of it here. In language people open up a space for interpretation by using vague, ambiguous words. Such

language ought to be deciphered by a listener and is called indirect language. There are quite a few metaphors for indirection such as "wrapped words"[3] or "veiled sentiments."[4] This technique of using indirect language is most prominent in societies that are egalitarian, avoid direct leadership,[5] and value an independence of mind. Here listeners are systematically given a freedom of interpretation that is substantial. Chard's floating plane of dots enticed the viewer to also take part in this field of tension and to briefly experience an indirect architectural mode. By looking through a floating plane separate from the pictorial image, perception becomes less direct and is highlighted as an independent, active element within the work. It is this obvious connection of Chard's dotted screens to the wider cultural debate about indirect communication and an autonomy of perception that distinguishes the A83 exhibit from Chard's earlier experiments with a floating world.

Bakhtinian scholars study indirect language and the post-structuralist space in which they operate. Does Chard inhabit that same space? Does he seem content with its architectural parameters, or the shape of that shared territory of meaning? Chard's spatial consciousness is a composite. It includes direct perception, ordinary photographic registration, but also perception as recollection. But that is just the beginning. He imagines his own role and that of his viewers, allowing people to take possession of spaces, through an architecture that tries to be generous. Chard's generosity fosters the capacity to wonder and to imagine far beyond the story that is being told, almost outside the narrative perimeter. This architect is interested in "diverting" that capacity, as his visual dilemmas implicate the observer in an active manner. In such sites of wonder and pleasure, you are not just looking at things that seem to fit in the world very well. Often things are taken apart from their context, with shadows or reflections out of place. Chard seems to have suspended the contexts that underpin a dialogic imagination. This is a reference to Bakhtin's essay "Discourse in the Novel" (1934–5)[6] and the back-and-forth movement between an object and its context that allows for a dialogue and construction of shared meanings. It is as if Chard has cut loose some of the threads that hold together that post-structuralist space, that shared territory. Perhaps one could imagine him using a grid to envelop the spatial parameters of post-structuralism? The space for dialogic meaning could be warped too, much like a diorama, diverted or poked from the inside to make space for wonder, tacit knowledge about uncertainty, a sense of unpredictability.

There are quite a few photos of Nat Chard on the floor with a camera taking pictures of ceilings. He finds elements of unpredictability within an existing architectural canon or spots a paradoxical shadow by a virtuoso Renaissance painter. His narrative includes many reference points— among others, the dioramas of the American painter and architect James Perry Wilson (1889–1976), the forensic techniques of the French biometrics researcher Alphonse Bertillon (1853– 1914), and the stereoscopic photos of the clouds of Mont Fuji by Masanao Abe, a Japanese physicist (1891–1966). This is an eclectic set of figures that keep Chard company on his exceptional journey. He asks me, "Have you ever seen a cactus out of place?" There you have it, he does it again, the certainty of context is taken away. He adds "you know, everything, wherever you put them, they seem to belong." How do you study and

deconstruct this belonging? Chard's recent "pre-architecture sketches" such as *Architectural Cactus*, *Architectural Beetle*, *Bored Cloud Case*, and *Witness* feature cactus-like elements and shapes that resemble beetle wings but could easily turn into cloud chambers. What seems to matter is that they are insect-like with a potential for composite visualization with polarized light. We are given a glimpse or an allusion to an architecture of a floating world in these sketches too. As stereoscopic optical viewers are given precedence, Chard introduces them to shifting and deconstructed contexts or simply a suspension of context, a floating out of context. Chard comments, "I hope it will do something, beyond what I hope it will do." ◰

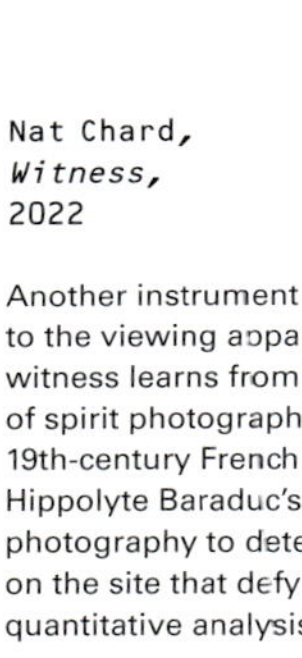

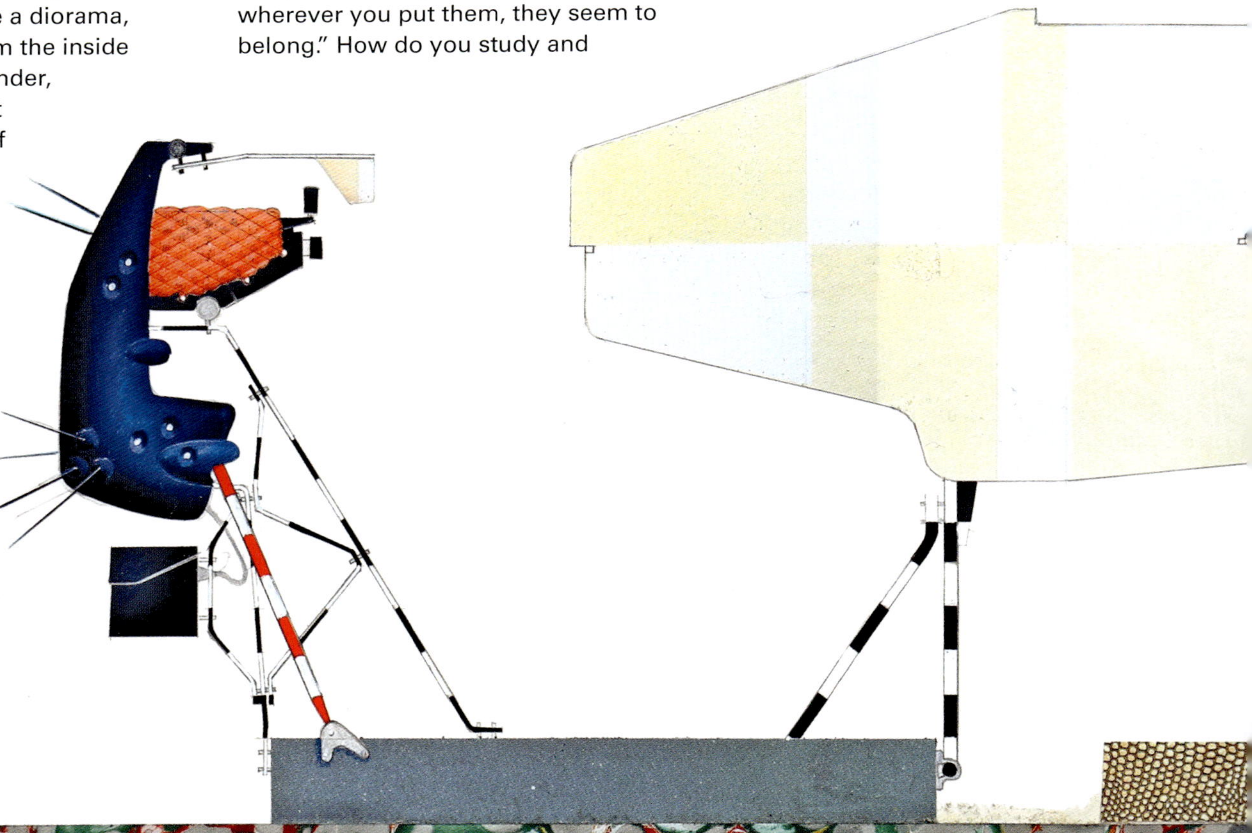

Nat Chard,
Witness,
2022

Another instrument related to the viewing apparatus, the witness learns from practices of spirit photography and 19th-century French physician Hippolyte Baraduc's fluidic photography to detect presences on the site that defy normal quantitative analysis.

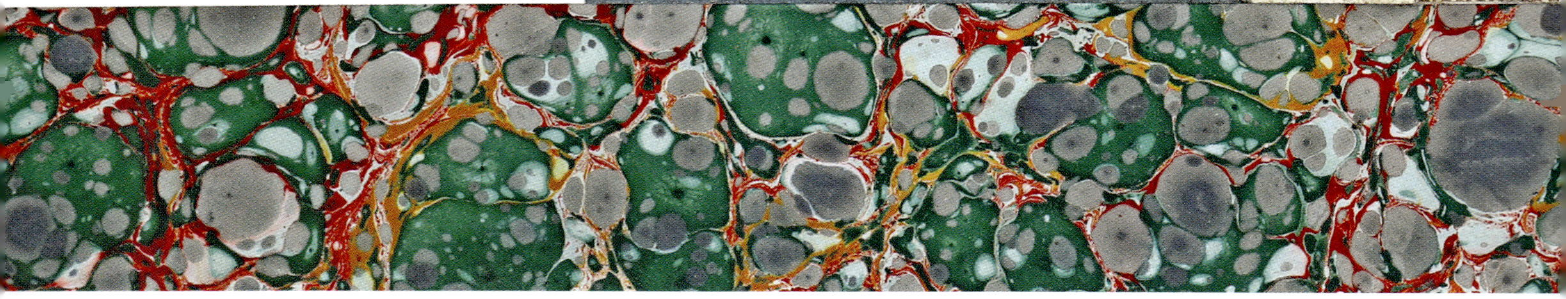

Nat Chard photographing one of Giovanni Battista Tiepolo's ceiling frescoes at the Würzburg Residence, Germany, 2017

The play between material and pictorial space has been a central motif in Chard's work. The study of Baroque ceiling paintings in relation to their host spaces, along with habitat dioramas in natural history museums, has provided substantial nutrition for his studies.

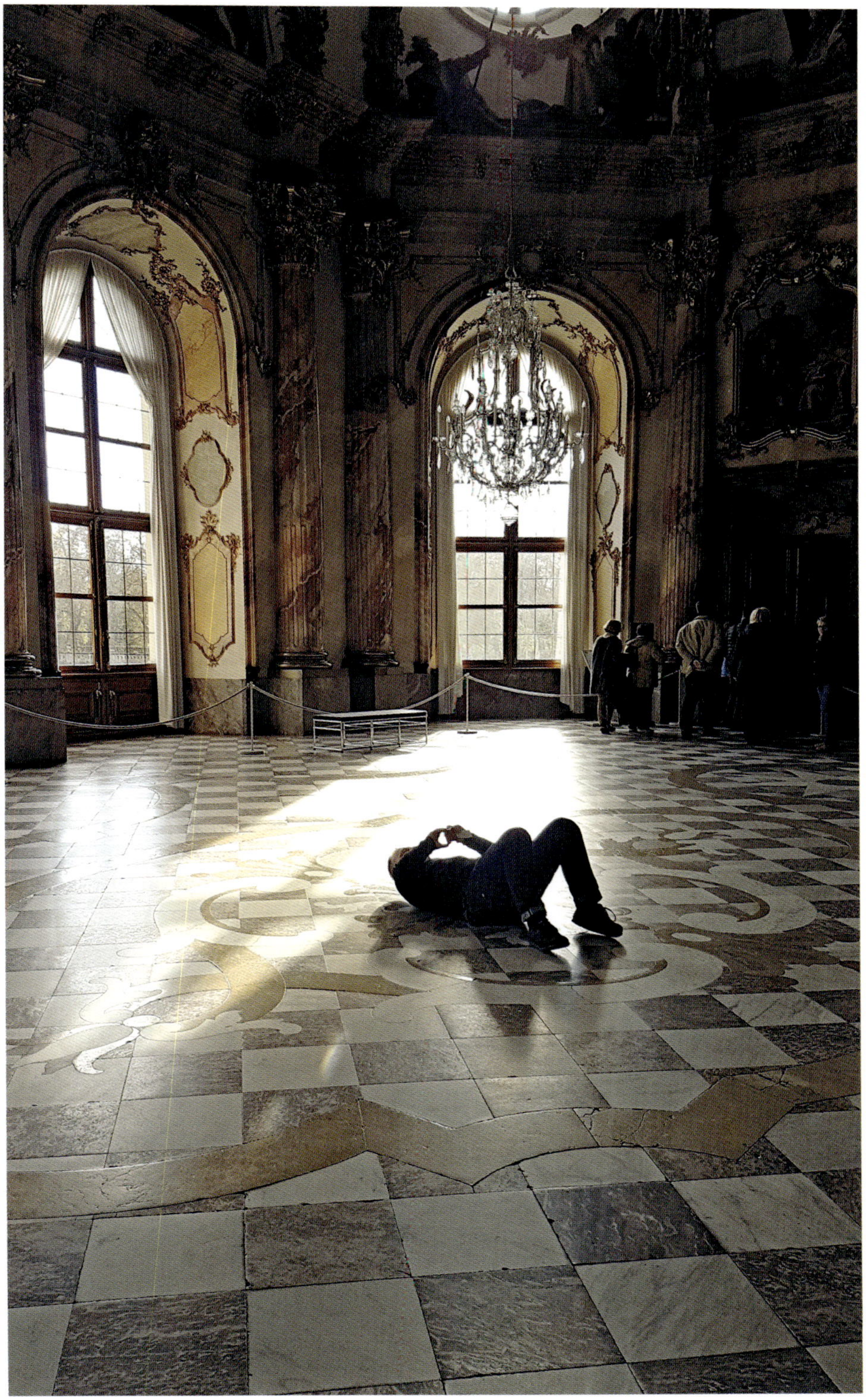

This article is based on a conversation between the author and Nat Chard on February 19, 2025.

Notes

1. See Donald Lawrence Brenneis, "Shared Territory: Audience, Indirection, and Meaning," *Text*, 6 (3), 1986, pp. 339–47.
2. Michael Polanyi, *The Tacit Dimension*, Doubleday & Company (Garden City, NY), 1966.
3. See Jane Monnig Atkinson, "Wrapped Words: Poetry and Politics Among the Wana of Central Sulawesi, Indonesia," in Donald Lawrence Brenneis and Fred R. Myers (eds), *Dangerous Words: Language and Politics in the Pacific*, New York University Press (New York), 1984.
4. See Lila Abu-Lughod, *Veiled Sentiments: Honor and Poetry in a Bedouin Society*, University of California Press (Berkeley, CA), 1986.
5. Donald Lawrence Brenneis, "Grog and Gossip in Bhatgaon: Style and Substance in Fiji Indian Conversation," *American Ethnologist*, 11 (3), 1984, pp. 487–506.
6. Mikhail Bakhtin, "Discourse in the Novel" [1934–5], tr. Caryl Emerson and Michael Holquist, in Michael Holquist (ed), *The Dialogic Imagination: Four Essays by Mikhail Bakhtin*, University of Texas Press (Austin, TX), 1981, pp. 259–421.

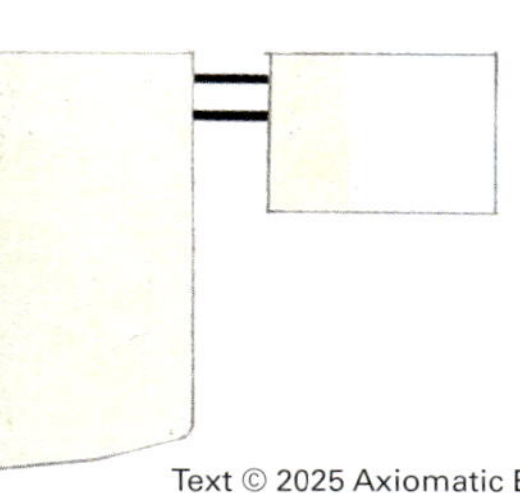

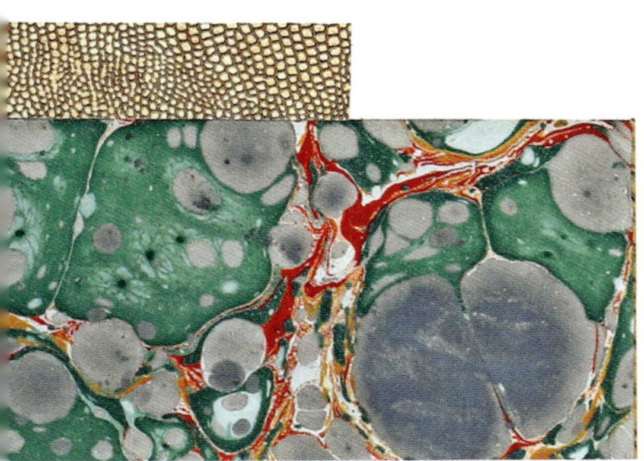

Resolution and Realism

Architect, teacher, and New Yorker Michael Young took a scan of A83's flat file room and a collage made by Michael Graves from the A83 archive as a point of departure. He combined this with works by Caravaggio to create a diptych of images that

Michael Young,
Paul Graves and *Peter Graves,*
diptych,
2024

Two composite images presented as a pair; above is *Paul Graves*, a photogrammetry scan of the basement of the A83 gallery archive basement overlaid with a scan of Caravaggio's *The Conversion of St. Paul* (1601) in the Cerasi Chapel, Rome. A small electrical outlet in the background and slats of wood in the foreground ground the composite image with some sense of

scale; and opposite, *Peter Graves*, an overlay of a frontal scan of Caravaggio's *The Crucifixion of St. Peter* (1601) from the Cerasi Chapel, with an oblique photogrammetry scan of Michael Graves's *Crooks House Collage* (1976) creates a composite with multiple vantage points from which a viewer could establish a relationship with the image.

A **Diptych** Iman Fayyad

Iman Fayyad

traverses space and time as a comment on modes of representation in art and architectural history. **Iman Fayyad,** an Assistant Professor of Architecture at the Harvard University Graduate School of Design, decodes these images.

In his 1917 essay "Art as Device", the Russian and Soviet literary theorist Viktor Shklovsky describes the "distancing effect" or "alienation effect" of a work of art,[1] channeling Karl Marx's theory[2] that a worker can feel estranged, or distant, from the objects of their production when that work reaches a level of complexity—manifested visually or technically—that crosses the threshold of comprehension or any meaningful association with the author. In the context of the state of architectural production today, this brings to mind the anthropologist Alfred Gell's essay "The Technology of Enchantment and the Enchantment of Technology" (1992),[3] in which he describes the technical virtuosity of art and its ability to thus enchant the viewer through the "halo-effect" of technical difficulty. He says, "The enchantment of technology is the power that technical processes have of casting a spell over us so that we see the real world in an enchanted form."[4] He argues that it is the "difficulty of access to an object which makes it valuable"[5]; that a viewer's inability to imagine the technical prowess required to produce intricate works of art makes them almost "magical," to use his term.

In an era where "realism, excessive realism, and digital hyperrealism"[6] are not only easily achieved but have simply become indices of the tools of contemporary architectural production—high-resolution 3D scanning, animation, VR/AR, digital fabrication—the intentional lack of resolution in Michael Young's composite images for the "Sixth Somewhat Annual Meeting" exhibition, hosted by the A83 gallery in New York in early 2025, serves as a pointed commentary on the value we place today on techniques of visual representation, archival material, collaborative authorship, and the physical artifact itself. Deliberately opaque, these layered images are created through some of the most sophisticated image-making processes, ones that can reproduce impressions of objects with remarkable precision. Yet the purpose of these prints is to convey neither accuracy nor clarity, or even technical prowess. Instead, they swap out complexity for messy complication; they celebrate misalignment, mismatches, and glitches, creating an effect of low resolution that would typically be a result of poor-quality scans, photographs, or resized raster images to fewer pixels.

The two prints—*Paul Graves* and *Peter Graves* (2024)—are composite montages from three different sources, presented in the A83 exhibition as a diptych. They are conflations of unrelated images—there is no commonality in the authors, locations, or times of their creation, content, and meaning, or techniques of production—but they each share a questioning of the relationship between realism and resolution. In art and philosophy, realism is often defined as a preoccupation with truthfulness, accuracy, objectivity, or the representation of the everyday; little is left to one's imagination. Young's experiments challenge this definition, particularly in the context of digital culture. The individual sources that make up the montages use technologies that attempt to re-create reality to as high a degree of accuracy as possible in digital images and three-dimensional models. Young processes these representations to a reduced resolution, but most importantly, conflates multiple truths with one another in a way that invents new, false realities.

One source is a photogrammetry point-cloud model of the flat-file archive room in the basement of A83 where a 1976 material collage, *Crooks Collage House*, by the late American architect, designer, and educator Michael Graves, is the focus point for the image scan; another is a photogrammetry point-cloud model of the Cerasi Chapel (1606) at Donato Bramante's and Gian Lorenzo Bernini's Santa Maria del Popolo in Rome (1477), where two Caravaggio paintings face each other, *The Conversion of St. Paul* and *The Crucifixion of St. Peter* (both 1601); and the last is a composite of two screenprints by the Bauhaus-influenced American artist David Roth—*Untitled 21* and *Untitled 23* (both 1979)—also from the archive of the A83 gallery.[7] According to Young, these images were experiments whose primary intent was to study the relationships between resolution and color in the translations between points of reflected energy, pixels of illuminated light, and dots of colored pigment.

A New Type of Image

Spanning centuries, geographies, and cultures, visual distortion has long been central to ideas about subjective bodily power and experience; the phenomenon has contributed profoundly to the relationship between space and painting as well as to image-making practices deeply rooted in the architectural discipline. The technique's applications range from Renaissance perspectivism and anamorphosis, to the orthographic perspective of Chinese painting, Islamic murals, and Cubism. Notably, the practice of quadratura (illusionist ceiling painting)—particularly in the frescoes of Baroque churches in Rome and elsewhere—cemented a new relationship between building, sculpture, and painting, fusing the projective qualities of the flat image with architectural form. Its greatest power and limitation, however, lie in the fusion of mind and body into a single, static position in space. At the same time, other techniques of trompe l'oeil in which painted characters spill outside of the architectural (and pictorial) frame, did not operate within precise mathematical constructs, relying

Michael Young,
Cerasi Chapel Point-cloud Model,
2023

below: Caravaggio's *The Conversion of St. Paul* and *The Crucifixion of St. Peter* face each other in the Cerasi Chapel in Rome. The viewer is only ever oblique to the two paintings, but their use in Young's composite images re-establishes their frontal relationship to the viewer.

Michael Young,
A83 Archive Point-cloud Model Montage,
2024

bottom: A point-cloud photogrammetry scan model has no definitive edge but simply diminishes in resolution and increases in distortion away from the focal point of the scan, in this case Michael Graves's *Crooks House Collage* on a pedestal.

Michael Young,
*David Roth, Composite
Montage,*
2024

below: A composite of several
screenprints by the artist
David Roth—*Untitled 21* (1979)
and *Untitled 23* (1979)—post-
processed and edited by Young.
Roth's prints predate the digital
but are reminiscent of the graphic
of pixelated screens.

Michael Young, *Paul Graves,*
"The Sixth Somewhat Annual
Meeting" exhibition, A83
gallery, New York, 2025

right: The screenprint of *Paul
Graves* on a square sheet as
displayed in the A83 gallery
for the exhibition. The square
boundary of the sheet (an
arguably agnostic shape) relieves
the medium of the print from
acknowledging the image's
complex relationship with
defining an edge condition or
definitive aspect ratio.

instead on a looser cognitive reaction to illusion. This was perhaps most famously practiced by Giovanni Battista Gaulli in his *Triumph of the Name of Jesus* (1661–79) in the vault of the nave at the Church of the Gesù in Rome.[8]

The diptych of composites created by Young evoke many of these historical ideas of visual narrative alongside the digital complexity of today's practices. Yet they offer a rather different take on the relationship between the viewing subject and the image. They borrow from various historical techniques in image-making practices that have contributed critically to architectural discourse over the centuries, particularly with regard to the relationship between flatness and three-dimensional space—chiaroscuro, perspective, anamorphosis, photography, and even quadratura. Each of the three individual elements that make up the composites has a distinct allegiance to flatness, staking their own claims to the limitations of flat media in representing spatial depth.

First, the material collage by Michael Graves is a three-dimensional sculptural object, framed like a (flat) painting or photograph. Second, the two Caravaggio paintings from the Cerasi Chapel are exemplars in the practice of chiaroscuro; conspicuously, these paintings are positioned in a strange way relative to one another as well as within the larger space of the church. They face each other in a small, niche-like chapel whereby the viewer is only ever oblique to the paintings and never frontal. Though they do not employ anamorphic techniques that allow the painting to perform spatially, they end up operating in a similar vein—positioning the viewer outside of the frame of the painting rather than within it, except in this case this relationship is forced by the physical restrictions of the space and not by the content of the painting itself. And finally, the pointillist screenprints by David Roth are reminiscent of pixels on malfunctioning digital screens; the presence of these prints in Young's composition is all-encompassing yet subtle, if noticeable at all. In fact, the Roth prints are indistinguishable and could be mistaken for some aesthetic effect of post-processing applied to the image as a whole.

Translating Resolution

Around since the mid-1800s, photogrammetry is a process of many projective translations. At its core, its purpose is to create three-dimensional information from two-dimensional data collected as light and color sources. By superimposing at least two photographs of an object or space taken from different angles, the photon data from the photographs is triangulated to create an interpolated mesh representing a three-dimensional facsimile of a space.

It is a process by which three-dimensional information is first flattened onto a two-dimensional plane, not as graphic points but as pixels of light and color. From there, this data is synthesized into a three-dimensional output. By definition, processes of translation typically imply the loss of information. Despite the increase in dimensionality that photogrammetry creates (from one- to two- to three dimensions), the resulting point-cloud data is, in fact, paradoxically a lower-resolution representation of the photographs used to create it. However, though it loses information, it creates new, synthetic data based on the limited information it has in two dimensions.

Young's *Paul Graves* and *Peter Graves* diptych presents several provocations and commentaries on the state of representation in architectural discourse today. Aside from questions of resolution, perhaps the most overt characteristic of these two images is that they challenge medium specificity in ways that even the most avant-garde image-making techniques struggle to tap into, especially more recent ones. They are digitally produced images, but were represented in the A83 gallery as screenprints and Risographs; they were created and viewed within the rectangular boundary of a digital screen and transferred physically onto square sheets of paper, though they themselves do not have a rectangular edge (or, arguably, any edge at all); they flatten highly three-dimensional representations (literally, in the case of the photogrammetry scans) onto a single view on only one plane. Young describes the process of photogrammetry as a projective system that cannot differentiate between surface and line; in other words, there is no distinction between edge and middle, periphery and center, and therefore no understanding of where contained space begins and ends.[9]

The prints' lack of a coherent edge boundary indicates that they are fragments of a larger field, highlighting the challenge of reducing a photogrammetry model into a representational medium that typically biases flatness, rectilinearity, and edges. As a result, a fragment of each Caravaggio painting is clipped seemingly arbitrarily, though likely in accordance with how shadow, light, and color appear in the painting itself. Photogrammetry scans work most effectively when lighting conditions in a space are even; the high contrast of chiaroscuro in the painting—a technique used, ironically, with the intention of adding realism to the scene—makes the scanning of it more difficult because of the contrast in light. In its high-resolution reproduction, therefore, it is not only less realistic, but less informative. The effect of the depicted figure in the image spilling out of its implied rectangular boundary is reminiscent of quadratura yet without the illusionistic effects.

The overlay of the Roth screenprints completes an image that is, in the end, not very legible but is a reminder that the entire composition, none of the contents of which acknowledge the frontality of the image, needs to preference a plane in its presentation as a static, singular image viewed either on a digital screen or a physical sheet of paper. In other words, the Roth overlays flatten and frame the composition. Otherwise, in *Peter* Graves, for example, the scan of the Graves collage is oblique to the front of the image on multiple planes; and the Caravaggio scan, paradoxically, re-establishes the viewer's frontal relationship to it, one that is not experienced even in the real space of the chapel.

It may be obvious by now, but worth stating explicitly, that these composites are all representations of physical matter. None of these images are digitally crafted, and yet their orthographic qualities are lost in their reinterpretation and reproduction as data points in digital media. As such, more than anything, Young's compositions offer a nostalgic nod not to what we have gained from our sophisticated digital tools, but rather what we have lost by removing ourselves from the physicality of printed matter. Especially recently, our engagement with physical objects tends to take place digitally and remotely. As much as the reproduction of objects at a high resolution attempts to replicate how we might encounter them physically, we still, nevertheless, experience them at a distance. Perhaps it is this deliberate loss of resolution that calls necessary attention to the retained value of the physical artifact despite the technological prowess of our digital media.

Returning to the idea of flatness, perspective, and the subject's relation to the painting, the composite images claim no predominant orientation for their viewing subjects, no dominant perspectival information, and no acknowledged frontality by any of its components. Although the layers of the images are reproductions of physical artifacts—objects that have real material qualities and dimensions—the only indication of scale and the only hint that these prints ultimately pay homage to an art archive in a real, physical space, is the appearance of an electrical outlet to the right of the Michael Graves print in *Paul Graves*. After all, despite their opacity, these images intend to reveal things that are concealed—the scan that contains the Graves collage is of the basement of the archives of the A83 printmaking studio, in preparation for an exhibition that celebrated prints by various practices the archive has stored or reproduced over the last several decades.

In *Peter Graves*, the figure of Michael Graves's collage rests obliquely in the foreground of the overall composition, akin to the skull in Hans Holbein the Younger's *The Ambassadors* (1533).[10] Like the skull, this figure, though not as eccentrically distorted, is similarly unrecognizable. However, unlike *The Ambassadors* or

the aforementioned perspectively distorted spaces and paintings, there is no vantage point from which any component of this print appears to be more or less coherent. Though intentionally engaged with real physical space, these prints are not necessarily interested in establishing a spatial relationship with a viewer. They may, instead, address an important question of where the future of image-making practices is headed; perhaps it is not visual, spatial, or cognitive in the same ways that our historical precedents cared to be. Rather, it may simply be about casting a different kind of relationship with the subject—one that is more introspective, reflexive, and, as Alfred Gell argues, is a way for art to establish social agency by engaging the viewer through enchantment. ◌

Notes

1. Viktor Shklovsky, *Theory of Prose*, tr. Benjamin Sher, Dalkey Archive Press (Champaign, IL), 1991, pp. 1–14.
2. Karl Marx, "Estranged Labor," in *Economic and Philosophic Manuscripts of 1844*, tr. and ed. Martin Milligan, Dover (Mineola, NY), 2007, pp. 67–83.
3. Alfred Gell, "The Technology of Enchantment and the Enchantment of Technology," in Jeremy Coote and Anthony Shelton (eds), *Anthropology, Art, and Aesthetics*, Clarendon Press (Oxford), 1992, pp. 40–64.
4. Ibid., p. 44.
5. Ibid., p. 42.
6. Mario Carpo, *The Second Digital Turn: Design Beyond Intelligence*, MIT Press (Cambridge, MA), 2017, p. 80.
7. Roth's work can be viewed at the Ro Gallery: www.rogallery.com/artists/david-roth/.
8. See https://artmuseum.princeton.edu/collections/objects/45004.
9. Michael Young, "Innovations in Distortion," *Design Ecologies*, 10 (1), 2021, p. 75.
10. See www.nationalgallery.org.uk/paintings/hans-holbein-the-younger-the-ambassadors.

Michael Young,
Graves Collage, Study 15,
2024

opposite: A photogrammetry scan of Graves's *Crooks House Collage* that was used in Young's *Paul Graves* and *Peter Graves* compositions.

Michael Young,
Graves Collage, Study 72,
2024

above: A photogrammetry scan of the framed Michael Graves work *Crooks House Collage* (1976) in the basement of the A83 printmaking studio. Various objects in the room, such as an electrical outlet and wood slats in the foreground, are mildly discernible, adding a sense of scale and realism to the image (realism in this case referring to the creation of an impression of a real space).

FROM ANOTHER PERSPECTIVE *A Word from AD Editor* **Neil Spiller**

Spaces for the Mind and Eye

James Kennedy

> The kind of painting which I find exciting is not necessarily representational or non-representational, but it is musical and architectural … Whether this visual relationship is slightly more or slightly less abstract is, for me, beside the point.
> — Ben Nicholson, "Notes on Abstract Art," 1941[1]

Artist James Kennedy was born in Northern Ireland in 1962 and educated at the Royal Scottish Academy of Music and Drama in Glasgow; the Rhodec Design Academy in Brighton, England, and the London School of Contemporary Dance. He now lives and works in New York. He is known for his drafting dexterity and his meticulous compositional and painting skills—usually in acrylic. This attention to detail produces layered works whose textured surfaces construct shallow relief/paintings—consisting of constellations of color, lines, planes, and fields that infinitely entertain and question the viewer's eyes.

Anatomical Fictions

During the mid-2010s, one of Kennedy's artistic preoccupations was depicting bodies in space. These falling, suspended, and trapped abstracted, often human, forms resonate with that other great modern painter and portrayer of human frailty and vulnerability, another Irishman, Francis Bacon. Kennedy's bodies, like Bacon's, are often caught and imprisoned in implied rooms and deformed, experiencing a continuing distortion that bends them out of shape. In Kennedy's case gravity seems to be an active force in such deformation. Backgrounds are often depicted in light mute colors that imply a ground, in both senses of the word, within which the figure is encased. Often the figures that aren't more abstract are shown in almost acrobatic poses, but there is a sense of jeopardy—though no heroism—as they hang upside down, caught in a moment of struggle against gravity.

James Kennedy,
Re-entry, "Anatomical Fictions" series,
2015

In the "Anatomical Fictions" series of paintings, bodies are suspended, caught, enclosed, disorientated, and extruded by gravity.

The Print

Kennedy rejoices, often, in the notion of the one-off, never-to-be-repeated original painting as an exceptional event in the world. In 2018 this was brought into question when he spent a month at Stoney Road Press in Dublin, Ireland, where he explored, for the first time, the notion of printing his paintings. This resulted in a set of four prints called "Transpositions." After this time, Kennedy commented, "As an artist, one always hopes that any expedition into another media will both expand and alter the language: and the plates and presses delivered on both of those fronts."[2] It was a cathartic, metamorphic moment for the artist, as the making of prints brings new nuances to the work—just as it has for all the architects also featured in this issue of ⌂. "I look at these prints and although they hold an essence of my 'Spatial' paintings, they are transported, rendered, made all the more visceral. I also hold draughtmanship [sic] in high esteem and feel that they impart a certain reverence for the craft."[3] The "Transpositions" suite reveals Kennedy's meticulous line work and brings his architectural use of void and mass to the fore.

James Kennedy,
My Own Mythology, "Anatomical
Fictions" series,
2019

opposite: Some figures in the series
are recognizably human; others
more abstract; some, like this one,
are a mixture of both. A self-portrait,
depicting a tentative escape perhaps?

James Kennedy,
Transnotation 2,
"Transpositions" series,
2020

left: A later example of the
"Transpositions" suite of prints, created
at Stoney Road Press in Dublin but
hand-finished with inks and acrylics
subsequently. It reveals Kennedy's
complex line work and drafting skills.

Reverences and Riffs

More recently Kennedy has moved away from the implication of the organic bodily figure in the foreground toward more abstract fields and frames that conjure all manner of associations. There is often enigma in the titles that can create a frisson between the painting and its name. *Superstructure*, *Ghost in the Machine*, *Vector Vertagonal*, *Bridge Component*, *Apparatus*, and *Suspension* are the names of some of Kennedy's paintings. Such nomenclature evokes an industrial vibe, yet the paintings often use fields of pastel colors (sometimes sparingly punctuated with primary colors), and they do not utilize the machinic metallic lexicon of structural engineering and componentry. At once a paradox is revealed. Paradox and almost pastoral, delightful ambiguity are everywhere and at every level in Kennedy's complete oeuvre. In late 2024 he exhibited a series of works at the Dolby Chadwick Gallery in San Francisco entitled "Crystalline Velocity,"[4] and these are no exception.

Vortex of Associations

Critics have remarked on a variety of precursors in art history with which Kennedy's work resonates. Indeed, Kennedy's art straddles but never plagiarizes these histories and movements. His thoughtful, ambiguous, enigmatic personal stylistic ways consistently win through to create a cornucopia of associations that confounds the viewer from making a definitive reading or attributing a single meaning to it. His process is one of discovery, not of predetermined artifice.

Some of the artistic approaches and methodologies that could be and have been used to attempt to uncover Kennedy's preoccupations are Futurism, Vorticism, Abstract Expressionism, the Romantic, colorful, swirling paintings of J.M.W. Turner, and the Modernist painter and sculptor Ben Nicholson. As architect and curator Mark Morris has written, "Kennedy has likened his works to landscapes, constructed sites that receive and negotiate architectural impositions … This palette of shape and Kennedy's method of juxtaposition also recalls the still-life Purist paintings of Le Corbusier."[5] Some have seen anger in the work and have surmised the painter's imperative to describe our contemporary world of confusion, aggression, and fragmented selves spiraling out of control. Others are entranced by the fragile beauty of the pieces—which describes a delicacy of interrelated parts, each lovingly articulated—as they visually drift in each work's formal vortex of associations. Morris continues, "Pattern is important to his work, as is craft and the character of line work: incised, dashed, floating on paint. The repetition of like elements, iterations of shape, and scaling of projected objects, pulls his larger works into the realm of murals."[6]

James Kennedy,
Apparatus,
2024

Kennedy's work is
undeniably architectural with
its emphasis on space. Often
architectures are implied by
his graphic and painterly
form-making.

Text © 2025 Axiomatic Editions.
Images: pp. 132–139 © James Kennedy

Architecture

For architects there is something undeniably architectonic about the paintings. They have the careful intent of architectural drawings and seek to describe worlds that are beyond architecture yet strangely connected to it. Sometimes plans and sections can be construed out of them, figure and ground can sometimes be fantasized, and perspectival spaces inhabited. They are a-scalar; detail and overall compositions coalesce, condensing into carefully juxtaposed wholes. Void and mass, light and dark, angular and curved, varied implied degrees of enclosure and occupation. Sometimes there is a figure that occupies a particular space or field in the overall vortex—whether implied, or explicit and forcibly colored and depicted, rising out of the picture plane and immediately catching the eye (all architectural tactics). Sometimes the figure is pseudo-anatomical, sometimes not. Human perception is based on our experience of our individual worlds—our universe of discourse. When we look at abstract forms, we seek to interpret them in tune with that experience, each differently. Boats, birds, bodies, fields, colors and delineation, paint contours, all contribute to a complex personal Rorschach test when reading the works.

A detail can become a painting with its own compositional protocols, so each macro painting can be perceived as a nesting of thousands of little micro paintings simultaneously inhabiting the surface. Sometime motifs repeat themselves to provide "scaffolding" or framing devices accentuating other areas. If we zoom out to consider each artwork as a whole, a sensation akin to flying over an alien patchwork quilt landscape manifests itself and a feeling of vertigo is often provoked. The most architectural of the "Crystalline Velocity" series is *Apparatus*, which implies a cluster of buildings seen in plan around a central void or atrium.

Face and Place

As English art critic, novelist, painter, and poet John Berger has written, "*Face*. Whatever the painter is looking for, he's looking for its face. All the search and the losing and the re-finding is about that isn't it? And 'its face' means what? He is looking for the return gaze and he's looking for its expression—a slight sign of its inner life."[7] Kennedy's work certainly has inner life, and one imagines the artist over the space of days and hours delicately searching for a painting's face until it returns his gaze and subsequently ours. There is another element to successful painting in Berger's mind: that of *Place*. "A place is where an event has taken or is taking place. The painter is continually trying to discover, to stumble upon, the place which will contain and surround his present act of painting. Ideally there should be as many places as there are paintings."[8] With every painting Kennedy creates a new place, discovering its geography and geomorphology as he goes about his business—revealing new worlds, a type of reverse archeology as he invents new terrain. ◬

Notes

1. Ben Nicholson, "Notes on Abstract Art," *Horizon*, October 1941; revised version in Herbert Read, "Introduction," *Ben Nicholson: Paintings, Reliefs, Drawings*, Lund Humphries (London), 1948.
2. www.stoneyroadpress.com/artists/james-kennedy.
3. Ibid.
4. James Kennedy, "Crystalline Velocity," Dolby Chadwick Gallery, San Francisco, November 14 to December 7, 2024.
5. Mark Morris, "James Kennedy: SHAPE-SHIFTING, An Invitational Exhibit," at John Hartell Gallery, Cornell University, Ithaca, New York, March 21 to April 29, 2016.
6. Ibid.
7. John Berger, *The Shape of a Pocket*, Bloomsbury (London), 2001, p. 27.
8. Ibid., pp. 28–9.

Stan Allen is an architect and George Dutton '27 Professor of Architecture at Princeton University, New Jersey, where he served as Dean of the School of Architecture from 2002 to 2012. He has realized buildings and urban projects in the US, South America, and Asia. His architectural work is published in his book *Points + Lines: Diagrams and Projects for the City* (Princeton Architectural Press, 1999) and his essays in *Practice: Architecture, Technique and Representation* (Routledge, 2008). He is co-editor of the volume *Landform Building: Architecture's New Terrain* (Lars Müller, 2011), and his most recent book is *Situated Objects: Buildings and Projects by Stan Allen* (Park Books, 2021).

Peter J. Baldwin is an architect, artist, and academic, and the Head of Architecture and the Built Environment at Birmingham City University, West Midlands, UK. Known for his experimental architectural drawings and his scholarship on representational practice, Peter's works have been widely exhibited and published and were recently included in Thom Mayne's "Impossible Drawings" exhibition at the A+D Museum, Los Angeles (2024) and "In Memoriam" at the Yale School of Architecture (2019). Peter's research has been published in *⌂ A Sublime Synthesis: Architecture and Art* (September/October, 2023) and *⌂ The Allegorical Architectural Machine* (November/December, 2024).

Greg Barton is a researcher and curator interested in spatial politics and museology. He has collaborated on a variety of projects with artists, architects, and activists, as well as institutions including the Canadian Centre for Architecture (CCA), Storefront for Art and Architecture, and Center for Architecture in New York. He studied at Columbia University Graduate School of Architecture, Planning and Preservation (GSAPP) and works in the office of Bernard Tschumi Architects coordinating archives, publications, and exhibitions.

Paddi Alice Benson is an architectural designer and researcher from London. She graduated from the Bartlett School of Architecture, University College London (UCL) with an MArch degree in 2017. For her undergraduate degree in architecture she studied at the University of Cambridge (2012), before completing a Master's in Music at the University of Limerick. In 2024 she concluded a PhD in Architecture by Design titled "(Mis)navigating Island *Topoi*" under Mark Dorrian and Adrian Hawker at the Edinburgh School of Architecture and Landscape Architecture (ESALA) at the University of Edinburgh, Scotland. Her research explored the island as a site of speculation, invention, and experimentation.

Bryan Cantley is an alumnus of the University of California, Los Angeles (UCLA) and the University of North Carolina at Charlotte. He is a Full Professor of Design at the California State University, Fullerton, and has been visiting faculty at the Southern California Institute of Architecture (SCI-Arc) and at Woodbury University in San Diego. His work is in the permanent collection of the San Francisco Museum of Modern Art (SFMOMA). He was the recipient of a Graham Foundation Grant in 2002. His work has been exhibited internationally, including in solo exhibitions. He was the International Guest Lecturer at the Bartlett School of Architecture, UCL, in 2008 and 2017. He has authored two books, *Mechudzu: New Rhetorics for Architecture* (Springer Verlag, 2011) and *Speculative Coolness: Architecture, Media, the Real, and the Virtual* (Routledge, 2023).

Nat Chard is Professor of Experimental Architecture at the Bartlett School of Architecture, UCL, following professorships at the Royal Danish Academy, Copenhagen; the University of Manitoba, Canada; and the University of Brighton, UK. He is an architect registered in the UK and has practiced in London. His work has been published and exhibited internationally. His research practice develops means of discussing uncertain conditions in architecture, and his recent work has been acted out through a series of drawing instruments.

Sir Peter Cook is a visionary British architect, co-founder of the influential Archigram group, known for conceptual works like *Plug-In City*. His built projects include Kunsthaus Graz in Austria, and two studios for Arts University Bournemouth in Poole, UK. A celebrated educator and writer, he has led institutions including the Bartlett School of Architecture, UCL, and the Institute of Contemporary Arts (ICA) in London. Knighted in 2007, he has taught globally and received numerous honors, including the RIBA Royal Gold Medal. His drawings are held in major collections worldwide. He leads the Peter Cook Studio of CRAB Lab, is a Partner at CBH Architects, and continues to shape architecture's future through design.

Adam Dayem is an architect and educator based in Brooklyn, New York. He is Assistant Professor at Rensselaer Polytechnic Institute School of Architecture, and a principal of Actual Office Architecture, a design practice that has received numerous awards for theoretical and built architecture. After graduating from Columbia University, he worked at Bernard Tschumi Architects on projects around the world including the New Acropolis Museum in Athens, Greece. His experimental architectural drawings have been included in group shows in the US and Europe. He is the editor of the book *Imaginary Wilds: Architectural Interventions for the Thomas Cole National Historic Site* (ORO Editions, 2024).

Iman Fayyad is an Assistant Professor of Architecture at the Harvard University Graduate School of Design (GSD) and founding director of projectif, an award-winning research design practice that explores relationships between projective geometry and the politics of physical space and building practice. Her work has been published in the *New York Times, Technology: Architecture and Design, Nexus Network Journal, Log,* and *Archinect*, and exhibited at the Carnegie Museum of Art in Pittsburgh, Pennsylvania, and the Roca Gallery in London. Her public built work and research on zero-waste geometric construction techniques has been widely recognized and funded.

Adrian Hawker is a graduate of the Mackintosh School of Architecture in Glasgow, Scotland, and the Architectural Association (AA) in London. His architectural designs, drawings, and constructs have been awarded, exhibited, and published internationally. He is Co-Director of Metis, an atelier for art, architecture, and urbanism founded with Mark Dorrian in 1997. He is a Senior Lecturer in Architecture and Contemporary Practice at the Edinburgh School of Architecture and Landscape Architecture (ESALA) at the University of Edinburgh, Scotland.

Jimenez Lai came of age in Canada, and lives in Los Angeles. Before establishing Bureau Spectacular, he lived in a desert shelter at Taliesin in Wisconsin and resided in a shipping container at Atelier Van Lieshout on the piers of Rotterdam, the Netherlands. His first book was *Citizens of No Place: An Architectural Graphic Novel* (Princeton Architectural Press, 2012). His work is in the permanent collections of the Museum of Modern Art (MoMA), New York; SFMOMA; the Art Institute of Chicago; and Los Angeles County Museum of Art (LACMA).

Jason Lee is partner and co-founder of tentwenty, a design research practice with an emphasis on the speculative intersection between landscape architecture and architecture, and Associate Professor of Architecture at Pratt Institute in New York. He has also taught at Columbia University and Cooper Union. His teaching and research cover a wide range of topics from new material practices with composites to the exploration of robotics and seamless tectonics, as well as ongoing design inquiries on the new civic via the lens of dirty realism.

CJ Lim is the Professor of Architecture and Urbanism at the Bartlett School of Architecture, UCL. He is the founder of CJ Lim Imaginarium, a creative academy fostering idiosyncratic imagination, and Studio 8 Architects, a UK-based multidisciplinary and international practice. His work explores how narratives from science fiction, history, socio-politics, and humanity can inform architecture and the innovation of resilient cities. A recipient of the Royal Academy of Arts London Grand Architecture Prize, he has authored 12 books including *Short Stories: London in Two-and-a-half Dimensions* (2011), *Smartcities, Resilient Landscapes + Eco-warriors* (2019), *Once Upon a China* (2021), and *Dreams + Disillusions* (2024), all published by Routledge.

Bea Martin is an architect, artist, and educator. She is a Senior Lecturer and researcher at the Manchester School of Architecture, and is currently undertaking a PhD in Architectural Design at the Bartlett School of Architecture, UCL. She is the founder of Speculative Assemblies, an experimental design lab that investigates the architectural image as a visual construct. As both a theorist and maker, her practice is rooted in a conceptual exploration—across digital and analog media—of the apparatus of drawing. Her work rigorously interrogates the role of drawing in architecture, treating it as both method and mission, sustained through continuous research and a deep commitment to craft. Her most recent exhibition was curated by Thom Mayne in Los Angeles.

Thom Mayne established Morphosis in 1972 as a collective practice engaged in architecture, urban planning, and design. The same year, he co-founded the Southern California Institute of Architecture (SCI-Arc). He has held teaching positions at UCLA, Columbia University, Yale University, Harvard University, the Bartlett School of Architecture, UCL, and many other institutions. He was awarded the Pritzker Prize in 2005 and the American Institute of Architects (AIA) Gold Medal in 2013. Between 2009 and 2016 he served on the President's Committee on the Arts and Humanities under President Obama. Morphosis has received over 120 AIA Awards and been featured in more than 30 monographs. The practice has been the subject of various exhibitions, including at the Centre Pompidou, Paris, in 2006.

Shaun Murray is a qualified architect and director of ENIAtype, a transdisciplinary architecture practice founded in 2011. He is Editor-in-Chief of *Design Ecologies*, an international peer-reviewed journal exploring architecture, technology, and philosophy. He earned his doctorate at the Planetary Collegium CAiiA Star, University of Plymouth. He is an Associate Professor at the Bartlett School of Architecture, UCL, and a Senior Lecturer at the University of Greenwich, London. Formerly a Unit Master at the Architectural Association (AA), he is the author of *Disturbing Territories* (Springer, 2006), and his innovative architectural drawings have been widely exhibited and published.

Owen Nichols is an architect, designer, curator, printmaker, and educator based in New York City. He is co-director of A83, a nonprofit architecture gallery, archive, and printmaking studio, where he has curated and designed over 20 exhibitions since its founding in 2020. He is also co-director of the architecture and design practice Chibbernoonie, featured in the US Pavilion at the 2025 Architecture Biennale in Venice. Nichols produced the printed matter in collaboration with participating architects for the *Sixth Somewhat Annual Meeting* at A83. He teaches at Cornell University and the Irwin S. Chanin School of Architecture at the Cooper Union.

Alex Pillen is an artist and anthropologist, and an Associate Professor in the Department of Anthropology at University College London (UCL). She regularly takes part in the crits of the X-25 unit at the Bartlett School of Architecture, UCL, taught by Nat Chard and Emma-Kate Matthews. Her essay "A Space That Will Never be Filled" was published in *Current Anthropology* in 2017. She is currently doing an MA in Contemporary Art Practice at the Royal College of Art (RCA), London.

Mark Smout and Laura Allen are professors based at the Bartlett School of Architecture, UCL, where they co-direct its Landscape Architecture Master's programs. Through their design research practice Smout Allen, they explore architecture's relationship with environmental and territorial change. Their teaching supports diverse, speculative agendas that bridge architecture with the humanities, sciences, and arts. Exhibited internationally, including at four Venice Architecture Biennales, their work combines conceptual design with innovative representation and passive systems. Their students regularly receive major awards, and their collaborations span institutions such as the University of Southern California (USC) Libraries, the British Council, and Williams F1. They are Honorary Fellows of the Royal Institute of British Architects (RIBA).

Neil Spiller is Editor of ⚐, and was previously Hawksmoor Chair of Architecture and Landscape and Deputy Pro Vice Chancellor at the University of Greenwich in London. Prior to this he was Vice Dean at the Bartlett School of Architecture, UCL. He has an international reputation as an architect, designer, artist, teacher, writer, and polemicist. His books include *Visionary Architecture: Blueprints of the Modern Imagination* (2006), *Digital Architecture Now* (2008), and *Architecture and Surrealism* (2016), all published by Thames & Hudson. He was also previously McHale Fellow, State University of New York at Buffalo, Visiting Professor at IUAV University of Venice, and Visiting Professor at Carleton University, Ottawa. He is the founding director of the Advanced Virtual and Technological Architecture Research (AVATAR) group, which continues to push the boundaries of architectural design and discourse in the face of the impact of 21st-century technologies.

Clara Syme is an architect, designer, curator, and educator based in New York City. She is co-director of A83, a nonprofit architecture gallery, archive, and printmaking studio, where she has curated and designed over 20 exhibitions since its founding in 2020. Syme is also co-director of the architecture and design practice Chibbernoonie, featured in the US Pavilion at the 2025 Architecture Biennale in Venice. Syme, along with Arnaud Hendrickx, designed the scenography for the *Sixth Somewhat Annual Meeting* exhibition at A83. She teaches at Cornell University and at the Irwin S. Chanin School of Architecture at the Cooper Union.

Bart Verschaffel is a philosopher and Emeritus Professor at the University of Ghent in Belgium. His publications on architectural theory, aesthetics, visual arts, and cultural philosophy include: *Charles Vandenhove: Architecture and Projects 1954–2014* (Lannoo Publishers, 2014); *Mock Humanity: Two Essays on James Ensor's Grotesques* (BAI, 2018); *What is Real, What is True? Picturing Figures and Faces* (Exhibitions International, 2021), *What Artistry Can Do: Essays on Art and Beauty* (Edinburgh University Press, 2022), and *Gezien de verte: Glossen bij kunst en esthetiek* (A&S/books, 2025). He curated the exhibitions: "Piranesi: The Print Collection of Ghent University" (Museum of Fine Arts Ghent, 2008/9); "b0b Van Reeth: Architect" (Palais des Beaux-Arts, Brussels, 2013); and "James Ensor and the Still Life in Belgium 1830–1930" (Mu.ZEE, Ostend, 2023/24).

Aleksandra Wagner is a psychoanalyst, and Professor Emerita at The New School in New York City. She is a training and supervising analyst and faculty at the city's National Psychological Association for Psychoanalysis (NPAP) and at the China American Psychoanalytic Alliance (CAPA). With Neil Spiller, she edited the ⚐ issue *Lebbeus Woods: Exquisite Experiments, Early Years* (March/April, 2024). She is the Executor of the Estate of Lebbeus Woods.

Michael Young is an Associate Professor and Coordinator of Graduate Studies at the Irwin S. Chanin School of Architecture at The Cooper Union. He is the author of *The Estranged Object* (Graham Foundation, 2015) and *Reality Modeled After Images* (Routledge, 2022). His practice Young & Ayata has received the Progressive Architecture Award, Design Vanguard Award, Young Architects Prize, AIANY Honor Award, and the 2025 Architecture Award from the American Academy of Arts & Letters. He was the recipient of the 2019–20 Rome Prize from the American Academy of Rome.

Founded in 1930, *Architectural Design* (⚎) is an influential and prestigious publication. It combines the currency and topicality of a newsstand journal with the rigor and production qualities of a book. With an almost unrivaled reputation worldwide, it is consistently at the forefront of cultural thought and design.

Issues of ⚎ are edited either by the journal's Editorial Director, Ashley Simone, and Editor, Neil Spiller, or by an invited Guest-Editor. Renowned for being at the leading edge of design and new technologies, ⚎ also covers themes as diverse as architectural history, the environment, interior design, landscape architecture, and urban design.

Provocative and pioneering, ⚎ inspires theoretical, creative, and technological advances. It questions the outcome of technical innovations as well as the far-reaching social, cultural, and environmental challenges that present themselves today.

For further information on ⚎, subscriptions, and purchasing single issues, visit: www.archdesignjournal.com

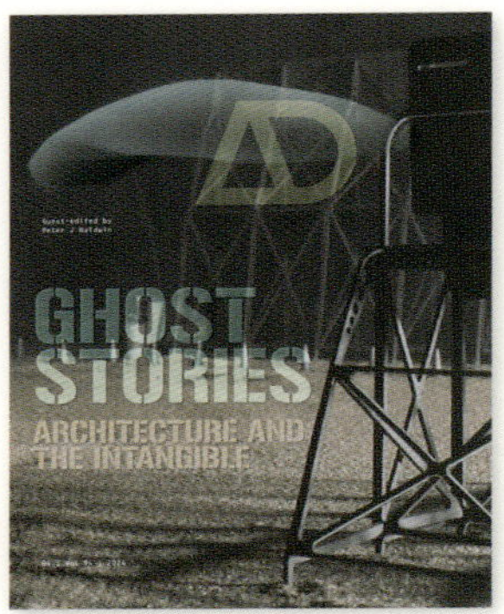

Volume 94 No 3
ISBN 978-1-394-19121-5

Volume 94 No 4
ISBN 978-1-394-18508-5

Volume 94 No 5
ISBN 978-1-394-23216-1

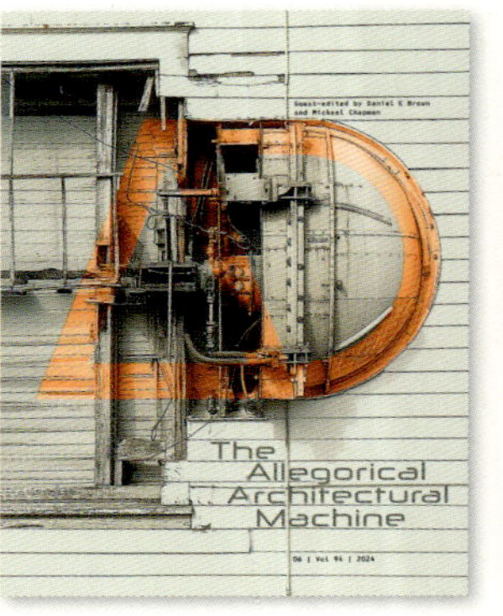

Volume 94 No 6
ISBN 978-1-394-20417-5

Volume 95 No 1
ISBN 978-1-961856-98-1

Volume 95 No 2
ISBN 978-1-961856-99-8